Spurgeon's Sermons
on
Proverbs

C. H. Spurgeon Resources

Spurgeon's Sermons on
Proverbs

CHARLES HADDON SPURGEON

kregel
PUBLICATIONS

Grand Rapids, MI 49501

Spurgeon's Sermons on Proverbs

Copyright © 1997 by Kregel Publications

Published by Kregel Publications, a division of Kregel, Inc., P.O. Box 2607, Grand Rapids, MI 49501. Kregel Publications provides trusted, biblical publications for Christian growth and service. Your comments and suggestions are valued.

For more information about Kregel Publications, visit our web site at http://www.kregel.com.

Cover artwork: Don Ellens
Cover and book design: Alan G. Hartman

Library of Congress Cataloging-in-Publication Data
Spurgeon, C. H. (Charles Haddon), 1834–1892.
    [Sermons on proverbs]
    Spurgeon's sermons on proverbs / Charles H. Spurgeon.
        p.   cm.—(C. H. Spurgeon sermon series)
    1. Bible. O.T. Proverbs—Sermons. 2. Baptists—Sermons. 3. Sermons, English. I. Title. II. Series: Spurgeon, C. H. (Charles Haddon), 1834–1892. C. H. Spurgeon sermon series.
BS1465.4.S68   1997   233'.706—dc21   96-53065
                                                                          CIP
ISBN 0-8254-3794-6

Printed in the United States of America

1 2 3 / 03 02 01 00 99 98 97

Contents

1

The Great Reservoir

Keep thy heart with all diligence; for out of it are the issues of life
(Proverbs 4:23).

If I should vainly attempt to fashion my discourse after lofty models, I should this morning compare the human heart to the ancient city of Thebes, out of whose hundred gates multitudes of warriors were wont to march. As was the city such were her armies, as was her inward strength, such were they who came forth of her. I might then urge the necessity of keeping the heart, because it is the metropolis of our manhood, the citadel and armory of our humanity. Let the chief fortress surrender to the enemy, and the occupation of the rest must be an easy task. Let the principal stronghold be possessed by evil, the whole land must be overrun thereby. Instead, however, of doing this, I shall attempt what possibly I may be able to perform, by a humble metaphor and a simple figure, which will be easily understood. I shall endeavor to set forth the wise man's doctrine that our life issues from the heart. Thus I shall labor to show the absolute necessity of keeping the heart with all diligence.

You have seen the great reservoirs provided by our water companies from which the water that is to supply hundreds of streets and thousands of houses is kept. Now, the heart is just the reservoir of man, and our life is allowed to flow in its proper season. That life may flow through different pipes—the mouth, the hand, the eye; but still all the issues of hand, of eye, of lip derive their source from the great fountain and central reservoir, the heart. Hence there is no difficulty in showing the great necessity that exists for keeping this reservoir, the heart, in a proper state and condition, since otherwise that which flows through the pipes must be tainted and corrupt. May the Holy Spirit now direct our meditations.

Mere moralists very often forget the heart and deal exclusively with

---

This sermon was taken from *The New Park Street Pulpit* and was preached on Sunday morning, February 21, 1858.

the lesser powers. Some of them say, "If a man's life be wrong it is better to alter the *principles* upon which his conduct is modeled: we had
better adopt another scheme of living; society must be remodeled, so
that man may have an opportunity for the display of virtues, and less
temptation to indulge in vice." It is as if when the reservoir was filled
with poisonous or polluted fluid some sage counselor should propose
that all the piping had better be taken up and fresh pipes laid down, so
that the water might run through fresh channels. But who does not perceive that it would be all in vain if the fountain-head were polluted
however good the channels. So in vain the rules by which men hope to
fashion their lives, in vain the regimen by which we seek to constrain
ourselves to the semblance of goodness unless the heart be right, the
very best scheme of life shall fall to the ground and fail to effect its design. Others say, "Well, if the life be wrong, it would be better to set the
understanding right. You must inform man's judgment, educate him,
teach him better, and when his head is well informed, then his life will
be improved." Now, *understanding* is, if I may use such a figure, the
stop-cock which controls the emotions, lets them flow on, or stops
them. It is as if some very wise man, when a reservoir had been poisoned, proposed that there should be a new person employed to turn the
water off or on in hope that the whole difficulty would thus be obviated.
If we followed his advice, if we found the wisest man in the world to
have the control of the fountain, Mr. Understanding would still be incapable of supplying us with healthy streams until we had first of all
purged the cistern whence they flowed.

The Arminian divine, too, sometimes suggests another way of im-
proving man's life. He deals with the *will*. He says, the will must first
of all be conquered, and if the will be right, then everything will be in
order. Now, *will* is like the great engine which forces the water out of
the fountain-head along the pipes so that it is made to flow into our
dwellings. The learned counselor proposes that there should be a new
steam engine employed to force the water along the pipes. "If," says he,
"we had the proper machinery for forcing the fluid, then all would be
well." No, sir, if the stream be poisonous, you may have axles to turn on
diamonds, have a machine that is made of gold, and a force as potent as
Omnipotence, but even then you have not accomplished your purpose
until you have cleansed the polluted fountain and purged the issues of
life which flow therefrom. The wise man in our text seems to say,
"Beware of misapplying your energies, be careful to begin in the right
place." It is very necessary the understanding should be right. It is quite
needful the will should have its proper predominance. It is very necessary that you should keep every part of man in a healthy condition.
"But," says he, "if you want to promote true holiness, you must begin

with the heart, for out of it are the issues of life. When you have purged it, when you have made its waters pure and limpid, then shall the current flow and bless the inhabitants with clear water. But not until then."

Here let us pause and ask the solemn and vital question, "Is my heart right in the sight of God?" For unless the inner man has been renewed by the grace of God through the Holy Spirit, our heart is full of rottenness, filth, and abominations. And if so, here must all our cleansing begin, if it be real and satisfactory. Unrenewed men, I beseech you ponder the words of an ancient Christian which I here repeat in your ear— "It is no matter what is the sign though an angel that hangs without, if the Devil and sin dwell within. New trimmings upon an old garment will not make it new, only give it a new appearance. Truly it is no good husbandry to bestow a great deal of cost in mending up an old suit that will soon drop to tatters and rags, when a little more might purchase a new one that is lasting. And is it not better to labor to get a new heart that all you do may be accepted, and you saved, than to lose all the pains you take in religion, and yourself also for want of it?"

Now, you who love the Lord, let me take you to the reservoir of your heart and urge upon you the great necessity of keeping the heart right, if you would have the streams of your life happy for yourselves and beneficial to others.

The Reservoir Must Be Full

First, keep the heart *full*. However pure the water may be in the central reservoir, it will not be possible for the company to provide us with an abundant supply of water unless the reservoir itself be full. An empty fountain will most assuredly beget empty pipes. Let the machinery be never so accurate, let everything else be well ordered; yet if that reservoir be dry, we may wait in vain for any of the water that we require. Now, you know many people (you are sure to meet with them in your own society and your own circle, for I know of no one so happy as to be without such acquaintances) whose lives are just dry, good-for-nothing emptinesses. They never accomplish anything. They have no mental force. They have no moral power. What they say, nobody thinks of noticing; what they do is scarcely ever imitated. We have known fathers whose moral force has been so despicable that even their children have scarcely been able to imitate them. Though imitation was strong enough in them, yet have they unconsciously felt, even in their childhood, that their father was, after all, but a child like themselves and had not grown to be a man. Do you not know many people who if they were to espouse a cause and have it entrusted to them would most certainly pilot it to shipwreck. Failure would be the total result. You could not use them as clerks in your office without feeling certain that

your business would be nearly murdered. If you were to employ them
to manage a concern for you, you would be sure they would manage to
spend all the money but could never produce a doit. If they were placed
in comfortable circumstances for a few months, they would go on
carelessly until all was gone. They are just the flats, preyed on by the
sharpers in the world. They have no manly strength, no power at all.

See these people in religion: it does not matter much what are their
doctrinal sentiments, it is quite certain they will never affect the minds of
others. Put them in the pulpit, they are the slaves of the deacons or else
they are overridden by the church. They never have an opinion of their
own, cannot come out with a thing. They have not the heart to say, "Such
a thing is, and I know it is." These men just live on. But as far as any util-
ity to the world is concerned, they might almost as well never have been
created, except it were to be fed upon by other people. Now, some say
that this is the fault of men's heads: "Such a one," they say, "could not get
on. He had a small head. It was clean impossible for him to prosper, his
head was small. He could not do anything. He had not enough force."
Now, that may be true. But I know what was truer still—he had gotten a
small heart and that heart was empty. For, mark you, a man's force in the
world, other things being equal, is just in the ratio of the force and
strength of his heart. A full-hearted man is always a powerful man. If he
be erroneous, then he is powerful for error. If the thing is in his heart, he
is sure to make it notorious, even though it may be a downright falsehood. Let a man be never so ignorant, still if his heart be full of love to a
cause, he becomes a powerful man for that object because he has gotten
heart-power, heart-force. A man may be deficient in many of the advan-
tages of education, in many of those niceties which are so much looked
upon in society; but once give him a good strong heart that beats hard,
and there is no mistake about his power. Let him have a heart that is right
full up to the brim with an object and that man will do the thing, or else
he will die gloriously defeated and will glory in his defeat.

HEART IS POWER. It is the emptiness of men's hearts that makes them
so feeble. Men do not feel what they are at. Now, the man in business
that goes heart and soul into his business is more likely to prosper than
anybody else. That is the preacher we want, the man that has a full soul.
Let him have a head—the more he knows the better; but, after all, give
him a big heart. When his heart beats, if his heart be full, it will, under
God, either make the hearts of his congregation beat after him or else
make them conscious that he is laboring hard to compel them to follow.
Oh! if we had more heart in our Master's service, how much more labor
we could endure. You are a Sunday school teacher, young man, and you
are complaining that you cannot get on in the Sunday school. Sir, the
service-pipe would give out plenty of water if the heart were full.

Perhaps you do not love your work. Oh, strive to love your work more, and then when your heart is full, you will go on well enough. "Oh," says the preacher, "I am weary of my work in preaching. I have little success. I find it a hard toil." The answer to that question is, "Your heart is not full of it, for if you loved preaching you would breathe preaching, feed upon preaching, and find a compulsion upon you to follow preaching. Your heart being full of the thing, you would be happy in the employment. Oh for a heart that is full and deep and broad! Find the man that has such a soul as that, and that is the man from whom the living waters shall flow to make the world glad with their refreshing streams.

Learn, then, the necessity of keeping the heart full. Let the necessity make you ask this question, "But how can I keep my heart full? How can my emotions be strong? How can I keep my desires burning and my zeal inflamed?" Christian! there is one text which will explain all this. "All my springs are in thee," said David. If you have all your springs in God, your heart will be full enough. If you do go to the foot of Calvary, there will your heart be bathed in love and gratitude. If you do frequent the vale of retirement and there talk with your God, it is there that your heart shall be full of calm resolve. If you go out with your Master to the hill of Olivet and with Him look down upon a wicked Jerusalem and weep over it with Him, then will your heart be full of love for never-dying souls. If you do continually draw your impulse, your life, the whole of your being from the Holy Spirit, without whom you can do nothing, and if you do live in close communion with Christ, there will be no fear of your having a dry heart. He who lives without prayer—he who lives with little prayer—he who seldom reads the Word—he who seldom looks up to heaven for a fresh influence from on high—he will be the man whose heart will become dry and barren. But he who calls in secret on his God—who spends much time in holy retirement—who delights to meditate on the words of the Most High—whose soul is given up to Christ—who delights in His fullness, rejoices in His all-sufficiency, prays for His second coming, and delights in the thought of His glorious advent—such a man, I say, must have an overflowing heart. As his heart is, such will his life be. It will be a full life; it will be a life that will speak from the sepulcher and wake the echoes of the future. "Keep thine heart with all diligence," and entreat the Holy Spirit to keep it full. Otherwise, the issues of your life will be feeble, shallow, and superficial; you may as well not have lived at all.

The Reservoir Must Be Pure

Second, it would be of little use for our water companies to keep their reservoirs full, if they did not also keep them *pure*. I remember to have read a complaint in the newspaper of a certain provincial town that a tradesman had been frequently supplied with fish from the water company, large eels having crept down the pipe and sometimes creatures a little more loathsome. We have known such a thing as water companies supplying us with solids when they ought to have given us nothing but pure crystal. Now, no one likes that. The reservoir should be kept pure and clean. Unless the water comes from a pure spring and is not impregnated with deleterious substances, however full the reservoir may be, the company will fail of satisfying or of benefiting its customers. Now it is essential for us to do with our hearts as the company must do with its reservoir. We must keep our hearts pure. If the heart be not pure, the life cannot be pure. It is quite impossible that it should be so. You see a man whose whole conversation is impure and unholy. When he speaks he lards his language with oaths. His mind is low and groveling. None but the things of unrighteousness are sweet to him, for he has no soul above the kennel and the dunghill. You meet with another man who understands enough to avoid violating the decencies of life. But still, at the same time he likes filthiness, any low joke, anything that will in some way stir unholy thoughts is just the thing that he desires. For the ways of God he has no relish. In God's house he finds no pleasure, in his Word no delight. What is the cause of this? Say some, it is because of his family connections—because of the situation in which he stands—because of his early education, and all that. No, no; the simple answer to that is the answer we gave to the other inquiry. The heart is not right. If the heart were pure, the life would be pure too. The unclean stream betrays the fountain. A valuable book of German parables by old Christian Scriver contains the following homely metaphor: "A drink was brought to Gotthold, which tasted of the vessel in which it had been contained; and this led him to observe. We have here an emblem of our thoughts, words, and works. Our heart is defiled by sin, and hence a taint of sinfulness cleaves unfortunately to everything we take in hand; and although, from the force of habit, this may be imperceptible to us, it does not escape the eye of the omniscient, holy, and righteous God." Whence come our carnality, covetousness, pride, sloth, and unbelief? Are they not all to be traced to the corruption of our hearts? When the hands of a clock move in an irregular manner, and when the bell strikes the wrong hour, be assured there is something wrong within. Oh how needful that the mainspring of our motives be in proper order, and the wheels in a right condition.

Ah! Christian keep your heart pure. You say, "How can I do this?" Well, there was of old a stream of Marah to which the thirsty pilgrims in the desert came to drink. When they came to taste it, it was so brackish that though their tongues were like torches and the roofs of their mouths were parched with heat, yet they could not drink of that bitter water. Do you remember the remedy which Moses prescribed? It is the remedy which we prescribe to you this morning. He took a certain tree cast it into the waters, and they became sweet and clear. Your heart is by nature like Marah's water, bitter and impure. There is a certain tree, you know its name, that tree on which the Savior hung, the cross. Take that tree, put it into your heart, and though it were even more impure than it is, that sweet cross applied by the Holy Spirit would soon transform it into its own nature and make it pure. Christ Jesus in the heart is the sweet purification. He is made to us *sanctification*. Elijah cast salt into the waters, but we must cast the blood of Jesus there. Once let us know and love Jesus, once let His cross become the object of our adoration and the theme of our delight, the heart will begin its cleansing and the life will become pure also. Oh! that we all did learn the sacred lesson of fixing the cross in the heart! Christian man! love your Savior more. Cry to the Holy Spirit that you may have more affection for Jesus and then, however gainful may be your sin, you will say with the poet,

> Now for the love I bear his name,
> What was my gain I count my loss;
> My former pride I call my shame,
> And nail my glory to his cross.

The cross in the heart is the purifier of the soul. It purges and it cleanses the chambers of the mind. Christian! keep your heart pure, "for out of it are the issues of life."

The Reservoir Need Not Be Peaceable,
but Not So with the Heart

In the third place, there is one thing to which our water companies need never pay much attention. That is to say, if their water be pure and the reservoir be full, they need not care to keep it *peaceable* and quiet, for let it be stirred to a storm, we should receive our water in just the same condition as usual. It is not so, however, with the heart. Unless the heart be kept peaceable, the life will not be happy. If calm does not reign over that inner lake within the soul which feeds the rivers of our life, the rivers themselves will always be in storm. Our outward acts until calmed always tell that they were born in tempests, by rolling in tempests themselves. Let us just understand this, *first*, with regard to ourselves. We all desire to lead a joyous life. The bright eye and the elastic foot are things which we each of us desire. To carry about a contented mind is that to which most men are continually aspiring. Let us all remember that the only way to keep our life peaceful and happy is to keep the heart at rest. Come poverty, come wealth, come honor, come shame, come plenty, or come scarcity, if the heart be quiet there will be happiness anywhere. But whatever the sunshine and the brightness, if the heart be troubled, the whole life must be troubled too.

There is a sweet story told in one of the German martyrologies well worth both my telling and your remembering. A holy martyr who had been kept for a long time in prison and had there exhibited to the wonderment of all who saw him the strongest constancy and patience, was at last, upon the day of his execution, brought out and tied to the stake preparatory to the lighting of the fire. While in this position, "he craved permission to speak once more to the judge, who was, according to the Swiss custom, required to be also present at the execution. After repeatedly refusing, the judge at last came forward when the peasant addressed him thus: 'You have this day condemned me to death. Now, I freely admit that I am a poor sinner, but positively deny that I am a heretic because from my heart I believe and confess all that is contained in the Apostles' Creed' (which he thereupon repeated from beginning to end). 'Now, then, sir,' he proceeded to say, 'I have but one last request to make; which is, that you will approach and place your hand, first upon my breast and then upon your own. Afterward, frankly and truthfully declare, before this assembled multitude which of the two, mine or yours, is beating most violently with fear and anxiety. For my part, I quit the world with alacrity and joy, to go and be with Christ, in whom I have always believed. What your feelings are at this moment is best known to yourself.' The judge could make no answer and commanded them instantly to light the pile. It was evident, however, from his looks that he was more afraid than the martyr."

Now, keep your heart right. Do not let it smite you. The Holy Spirit says of David, "David's heart smote him." The smiting of the heart is more painful to a good man, than the rough blows of the fist. It is a blow that can be felt; it is iron that enters into the soul. Keep your heart in good temper. Do not let that get fighting with you. Seek that the peace of God which passes all understanding may keep your heart and mind through Christ Jesus. Bend your knee at night, and with a full confession of sin, express your faith in Christ, then you may "dread the grave as little as your bed." Rise in the morning and give your heart to God. Put the sweet angels of perfect love and holy faith therein, and you may go into the world. Were it full of lions and of tigers, you would no more need to dread it than Daniel when he was cast into the lion's den. Keep the heart peaceable and your life will be happy.

Remember, in the *second* place, that it is just the same with regard to other men. I should hope we all wish to lead quiet lives, and as much as lies in us to live peaceably with all men. There is a particular breed of men—I do not know where they come from, but they are mixed up now with the English race and to be met with here and there—men who seem to be born for no other reason whatever but to fight—always quarreling and never pleased. They say that all Englishmen are a little that way—that we are never happy unless we have something to grumble at. They say the worst thing that ever could be done with us would be to give us some entertainment at which we could not grumble, because we should be mortally offended because we had not the opportunity of displaying our English propensities. I do not know whether that is true of us all, but it is true of some. You cannot sit with them in a room but they introduce a topic upon which you are quite certain to disagree with them. You could not walk with them half a mile along the public streets but they would be sure to make an observation against everybody and everything they saw. They talk about ministers: one man's doctrine is too high, another's is too low. One man they think is a great deal too effeminate and precise, another they say is so vulgar they would not hear him at all. They say of another man that they do not think he attends to visiting his people; of another, that he visits so much that he never prepares for the pulpit. No one can be right for them.

Why is this? Whence arises this continual snarling? The heart must again supply the answer. They are morose and sullen in the inward parts and hence their speech betrays them. They have not had their hearts brought to feel that God has made of one blood all nations that dwell upon the face of the earth. If they have felt that, they have never been brought to spell in their hearts—"By this shall all men know that ye are my disciples, if ye love one another." Whichever may have been put there of the other ten, the eleventh commandment was never written there. "A new commandment give I unto you, that ye love one another." That they forgot. Oh! dear Christian people, seek to have your hearts full of love. If you have had little hearts until now that could not hold love enough for more than your own denomination, get your hearts enlarged so that you may have enough to send out service pipes to all God's people throughout the habitable globe. Then whenever you meet a man who is a true-born heir of heaven he has nothing to do but to turn the tap, and out of your loving heart will begin to flow issues of true, fervent, unconstrained, willing, living love. Keep your heart peaceable that your life may be so. For out of the heart are the issues of life.

How is this to be done? We reply again, we must ask the Holy Spirit to pacify the heart. No voice but that which on Galilee's lake said to the storm, "Be still," can ever lay the troubled waters of a stormy heart. No strength but Omnipotence can still the tempest of human nature. Cry out mightily to Him. He still sleeps in the vessel with His church. Ask him to awake, lest your piety should perish in the waters of contention. Cry to Him that He may give your heart peace and happiness. Then shall your life be peaceful, spend it where you may, in trouble or in joy.

A Reservoir Must Not Be Divided

A little further. When the water-works company has gathered an abundance of water in the reservoir, there is one thing they must always attend to: that is, they must take care they do not attempt too much, or otherwise they will fail. Suppose they lay on a great main pipe in one place to serve one city and another main pipe to serve another, and the supply which was intended to fill one channel is diverted into a score of streams, what would be the result? Why nothing would be done well, but everyone would have cause to complain. Now, man's heart is after all so little that there is only one great direction in which its living water can ever flow. My fourth piece of advice to you from this text is, Keep your heart *undivided*.

Suppose you see a lake, and there are twenty or thirty streamlets running from it. Why, there will not be one strong river in the whole country. There will be a number of little brooks which will be dried up in the summer and will be temporary torrents in the winter. They will every one of them be useless for any great purposes because there is not water enough in the lake to feed more than one great stream. Now, a man's heart has only enough life in it to pursue one object fully. You must not give half your love to Christ and the other half to the world. No man can serve God and mammon because there is not enough life in the heart to serve the two. Alas! many people try this, and they fail both ways.

I have known a man who has tried to let some of his heart run into the world, and another part he allowed to drip into the church. The effect has been this: when he came into the church he was suspected of hypocrisy. "Why," they said, "if he were truly with us, could he have done yesterday what he did, and then come and profess so much today?" The church looks upon him as a suspicious one. Or, if he deceives them, they feel he is not of much use to them because they have not gotten all his heart. What is the effect of his conduct in the world? Why, his religion is a fetter to him there. The world will not have him, and the church will not have him. He wants to go between the two and both despise him. I never saw anybody try to walk on both sides of the street but a drunken man. *He* tried it, and it was very awkward work indeed. But I have seen many people in a moral point of view try to walk on both sides of the street. I thought there was some kind of intoxication in them or else they would have given it up as a very foolish thing.

Now, if I thought this world and the pleasures thereof worth my seeking, I would just seek them and go after them. I would not pretend to be religious. But if Christ be Christ, and if God be God, let us give our whole hearts to Him and not go shares with the world. Many a church member manages to walk on both sides of the street in the following manner: His sun is very low indeed—it has not much light, not much heat, and is come almost to its setting. Now sinking suns cast long shadows, and this man stands on the world's side of the street and casts a long shadow right across the road to the opposite side of the wall just across the pavement. Aye, it is all we get with many of you. You come and you take the sacramental bread and wine. You are baptized. You join the church. What we get is just your shadow. There is your substance on the other side of the street, after all. What is the good of the empty chrysalis of a man? And yet many of our church members are little better. They just do as the snake does that leaves its slough behind. They give us their slough, their skin, the chrysalis case in which life once was, and then they go themselves hither and thither after their own wanton wills. They give us the outward, and then give the world the inward. O how foolish this, Christian! Your master gave Himself wholly for you; give yourself unreservedly to Him. Keep not back part of the price. Make a full surrender of every motion of your heart. Labor to have but one object and one aim. And for this purpose give God the keeping of your heart. Cry out for more of the divine influences of the Holy Spirit so that when your soul is preserved and protected by Him, it may be directed into one channel, and one only, that your life may run deep and pure, and clear and peaceful. Its only banks being God's will, its only channel the love of Christ and a desire to please Him.

Thus wrote Spencer in days long gone by: "Indeed, by nature, man's heart is a very divided, broken thing, scattered and parceled out, a piece to this creature, and a piece to that lust. One while this vanity hires him, (as Leah did Jacob of Rachel,) anon when he hath done some drudgery for that, he lets out himself to another: thus divided is man and his affections. Now the elect, when God hath decreed to be vessels of honour, consecrated for his holy use and service, he throws into the fire of his word, that being there softened and melted, he may by his transforming Spirit cast them anew, as it were, into a holy oneness so that he who before was divided from God, and lost among the creatures, and his lusts, that shared him among them, now, his heart is gathered into God from them all; it looks with a single eye on God, and acts for him in all that he doth: if therefore thou wouldest know whether thy heart be sincere, inquire whether it be thus made anew."

Reservoirs of Wine

Now, my last point is rather a strange one perhaps. Once upon a time, when one of our kings came back from a captivity, old historians tell us that there were fountains in Cheapside that did run with wine. So bounteous was the king, and so glad the people, that instead of water they made wine flow free to everybody. There is a way of making our life so rich, so full, so blessed to our fellow men that the metaphor may be applicable to us, and men may say that our life flows with wine when other men's lives flow with water. You have known some such men. There was a Howard. John Howard's life was not like our poor common lives. He was so benevolent, his sympathy with the race so self-denying, that the streams of his life were like generous wine. You have known another, an eminent saint, one who lived very near to Jesus. When you talked yourself, you felt your conversation was poor watery stuff. But when He talked to you, there was an unction and a savor about His words, a solidity and a strength about His utterances which you could appreciate, though you could not attain to it. You have sometimes said, "I wish my words were as full, as sweet, as mellow, and as unctuous as the words of such a one! Oh! I wish my actions were just as rich, had as deep a color, and as pure a taste as the acts of so-and-so. All I can do seems but little and empty when compared with His high attainments. Oh, that I could do more! Oh, that I could send streams of pure gold into every house instead of my poor dross." Well, Christian, this should teach you to keep your heart full of rich things. Never, never neglect the Word of God. That will make your heart rich with precept, rich with understanding. Then your conversation, when it flows from your mouth, will be like your heart, rich, unctuous, and savory. Make your heart full of rich, generous love, and then the stream that flows from your hand will be just as rich and generous as your heart. Above all, get Jesus to live in your heart, and then out of your belly shall flow rivers of living water, more rich, more satisfying than the water of the well of Sychar of which Jacob drank. Oh go, Christian, to the great mine of riches and cry to the Holy Spirit to make your heart rich to salvation. So shall your life and conversation be a boon to your fellows. When they see you, your face shall be as the angel of God. You shall wash your feet in butter and your steps in oil. They that sit in the gate shall rise up when they see you, and men shall do you reverence.

But one single sentence, and we have done. Some of your hearts are not worth keeping. The sooner you get rid of them the better. They are hearts of stone. Do you feel today that you have a stony heart? Go home, and I pray the Lord hear my desire that your polluted heart may be removed. Cry to God and say, "Take away my heart of stone and give me a heart of flesh." A stony heart is an impure heart, a divided heart, an unpeaceful heart. It is a heart that is poor and poverty-stricken, a heart that is void of all goodness, and you cannot neither bless yourself nor others if your heart be such. O Lord Jesus! will you be pleased this day to renew many hearts? Will you break the rock in pieces and put flesh instead of stone, and you shall have the glory, world without end!

2
The Talking Book

When thou awakest, it shall talk with thee (Proverbs 6:22).

It is a very happy circumstance when the commandment of our father and the law of our mother are also the commandment of God and the law of the Lord. Happy are they who have a double force to draw them to the right—the bonds of nature, and the cords of grace. They sin with a vengeance who sin both against a father on earth and the great Father in heaven. They exhibit a virulence and a violence of sin who do despite to the tender obligations of childhood, as well as to the demands of conscience and God. Solomon, in the passage before us, evidently speaks of those who find in the parents' law and in God's law the same thing, and he admonishes such to bind the law of God about their hearts and to tie it about their necks; by which he intends inward affection and open avowal. The law of God should be so dear to us that it should be bound about the most vital organ of our being, braided about our heart. That which a man carries in his hand he may forget and lose, that which he wears upon his person may be torn from him, but that which is bound about his heart will remain there as long as life remains. We are to love the Word of God with all our heart, and mind, and soul, and strength. With the full force of our nature we are to embrace it. All our warmest affections are to be bound up with it. When the wise man tells us, also, to wear it about our necks, he means that we are never to be ashamed of it. No blush is to mantle our cheek when we are called Christians. We are never to speak with bated breath in any company concerning the things of God. Manfully must we take up the cross of Christ. Cheerfully must we avow ourselves to belong to those who have respect to the divine testimonies. Let us count true religion to be our highest ornament. As magistrates put upon them their gold

---

This sermon was taken from *The Metropolitan Tabernacle Pulpit* and was preached on Sunday morning, October 22, 1871.

chains and think themselves adorned thereby, so let us tie about our
necks the commands and the Gospel of the Lord our God.

In order that we may be persuaded so to do, Solomon gives us three
telling reasons. He says that God's law, by which I understand the
whole run of Scripture, and, especially the Gospel of Jesus Christ, will
be a guide to us: "When thou goest, it shall lead thee." It will be a
guardian to us: "When thou sleepest"—when you are defenseless and
off your guard—"it shall keep thee." And it shall also be a dear companion to us: "When thou awakest, it shall talk with thee." Any one of
these three arguments might surely suffice to make us seek a nearer acquaintance with the sacred Word. We all need a *guide,* for "it is not in
man that walketh to direct his steps." Left to our own ways, we soon
excel in folly. There are dilemmas in all lives where a guide is more
precious than a wedge of gold. The Word of God, as an infallible direc-
tor for human life, should be sought by us and will lead us in the highway of safety. Equally powerful is the second reason: the Word of God
will become the *guardian* of our days. Whosoever hearkens to it shall
dwell safely and shall be quiet from fear of evil. Unguarded moments
there may be. Times, inevitable to our imperfection, there will be,
when, unless some other power protect us, we shall fall into the hands
of the foe. Blessed is he who has God's law so written on his heart, and
wears it so about his neck as armor of proof, that at all times he is in-
vulnerable, kept by the power of God through faith to salvation.

But I prefer, this morning, to keep to the third reason for loving
God's Word. It is this: that it becomes *our sweet companion:* "When
thou awakest, it shall talk with thee." The inspired law of God which
David in the hundred and nineteenth Psalm calls God's testimonies,
precepts, statutes, and the life is the friend of the righteous. Its essence
and marrow is the Gospel of Jesus, the law-fulfiller, and this also is the
special solace of believers. Of the whole sacred volume it may be said,
"When thou awakest, it shall talk with thee." I gather four or five
thoughts from this expression and upon these we will speak.

The Word Is Living

We perceive here that the Word is living. How else could it be said:
"It shall talk with thee"? A dead book cannot talk nor can a dumb book
speak. It is clearly a living book, then, and a speaking book: "The word
of God, which liveth and abideth for ever." How many of us have found
this to be most certainly true! A large proportion of human books are
long ago dead and even shriveled like Egyptian mummies. The mere
course of years has rendered them worthless, their teaching is dis-
proved, and they have no life for us. Entomb them in your public li-
braries if you will, but, henceforth, they will stir no man's pulse and

warm no man's heart. But this thrice blessed book of God, though it has been extant among us these many hundreds of years, is immortal in its life, unwithering in its strength. The dew of its youth is still upon it. Its speech still drops as the rain fresh from heaven. Its truths are overflowing founts of ever fresh consolation. Never a book spoke like this book. Its voice, like the voice of God, is powerful and full of majesty.

Whence comes it that the Word of God is living? Is it not, first, because *it is pure truth?* Error is death, truth is life. No matter how well established an error may be by philosophy or by force of arms or the current of human thought, the day comes that shall burn as an oven and all untruth shall be as stubble before the fire. The tooth of time devours all lies. Falsehoods are soon cut down, and they wither as the green herb. Truth never dies, it dates its origin from the immortals. Kindled at the source of light, its flame cannot be quenched. If by persecution it be for a time covered, it shall blaze forth anew to take reprisals upon its adversaries. Many a once venerated system of error now rots in the dead past among the tombs of the forgotten. But the truth as it is in Jesus knows no sepulcher and fears no funeral. It lives on, and must live while the Eternal fills his throne.

The Word of God is living, because *it is the utterance of an immutable, self-existing God.* God does not speak today what He meant not yesterday, neither will He tomorrow blot out what He records today. When I read a promise spoken three thousand years ago, it is as fresh as though it fell from the eternal lips today. There are, indeed, no dates to the Divine promises. They are not of private interpretation, nor to be monopolized by any generation. I say again, as fresh today the eternal Word drops from the Almighty's lips as when He uttered it to Moses or to Elias, or spoke it by the tongue of Esaias or Jeremiah. The Word is always sure, steadfast, and full of power. It is never out of date. Scripture bubbles up evermore with good matters, it is an eternal Geyser, a spiritual Niagara of grace, forever falling, flashing, and flowing on. It is never stagnant, never brackish or defiled, but always clear, crystal, fresh, and refreshing; so, therefore, ever living.

The Word lives, again, because *it enshrines the living heart of Christ.* The heart of Christ is the most living of all existences. It was once pierced with a spear, but it lives on and yearns toward sinners. It is as tender and compassionate as in the days of the Redeemer's flesh. Jesus, the Sinner's Friend, walks in the avenues of Scripture as once He traversed the plains and hills of Palestine. You can see Him still, if you have opened eyes, in the ancient prophecies. You can behold Him more clearly in the devout evangelists. He opens and lays bare His inmost soul to you in the epistles and makes you hear the footsteps of His approaching advent in the symbols of the Apocalypse. The living Christ is

in the Book. You behold His face in almost every page. Consequently, it
is a Book that can talk. The Christ of the mount of benedictions speaks
in it still. The God who said, "Let there be light," gives forth from its
pages the same divine fiat. While the incorruptible truth, which saturated every line and syllable of it when first it was penned, abides
therein in full force and preserves it from the finger of decay. "The
grass withereth, and the flower thereof falleth away: but the word of the
Lord endureth forever."

Over and above all this, *the Holy Spirit has a peculiar connection
with the word of God.* I know that He works in the ministries of all His
servants whom He has ordained to preach. But for the most part, I have
remarked that the work of the Spirit of God in men's hearts is rather in
connection with the text we quote than with our explanations of them.
"Depend upon it," says a deeply spiritual writer, "it is God's word, not
man's comment on it, which saves souls." God does save souls by our
comment, but still it is true that the majority of conversions have been
wrought by the agency of a text of Scripture. It is the Word of God that
is living and powerful and sharper than any two-edged sword. There
must be life in it, for by it men are born again. As for believers, the Holy
Spirit often sets the Word on a blaze while they are studying it. The letters were at one time before us as mere letters, but the Holy Spirit suddenly came upon them, and they spoke with tongues. The chapter is
lowly as the bush at Horeb, but the Spirit descends upon it, and lo! it
glows with celestial splender—God appearing in the words, so that we
feel like Moses when he put off his shoes from his feet because the place
whereon he stood was holy ground. It is true, the mass of readers understand not this and look upon the Bible as a common book. But if they
understand it not, at least let them allow the truthfulness of our assertion
when we declare that hundreds of times we have as surely felt the presence of God in the page of Scripture as ever Elijah did when he heard
the Lord speaking in a still small voice. The Bible has often appeared to
us as temple God, and the posts of its doors have moved at the voice of
him that cried, whose train also has filled the temple. We have been con-
strained adoringly to cry with the seraphim, "Holy, holy, holy, is the
Lord God of Hosts." The Jews place as a frontispiece to their great Bible
the text, "Surely God is in this place; it is none other than the house of
God, and the very gate of heaven." And they say well. It is, indeed, a
spiritual temple, a most holy house, garnished with precious stones for
beauty and overlaid within and without with pure gold, having for its
chief glory the presence of the Lord, so gloriously revealed that, oftentimes, the priests of the Lord cannot stand to minister by reason of the
glory of the Lord which fills the house. God the Holy Spirit vivifies the
letter with His presence, and then it is to us a living word indeed.

And now, dear friends, if these things be so—and our experience certifies them—let us take care how we trifle with a book that is so instinct with life. Might not many of you remember your faults this day were we to ask you whether you are habitual students of holy writ? Readers of it I believe you are. But are you searchers, for the promise is not to those who merely read, but to those who delight in sitting at the feet of Jesus with his Word as their schoolbook? If not, remember, though you may be saved, you lack very much of the blessing which otherwise you might enjoy. Have you been backsliding? Refresh your soul by meditating in the divine statues, and you will say with David "Thy word hath quickened me." Are you faint and weary? Go and talk with this living book. It will give you back your energy, and you shall mount again as with the wings of eagles. But are you unconverted altogether? Then I cannot direct you to Bible reading as being the way of salvation, nor speak of it as though it had any merit in it. But I would, nevertheless, urge upon you unconverted people great reverence for Scripture, an intimate acquaintance with its contents, and a frequent perusal of its pages, for it has occurred ten thousand times over that when men have been studying the Word of Life, the Word has brought life to them. "The entrance of thy word giveth light." Like Elijah and the dead child, the Word has stretched itself upon them, and their dead souls have been made to live. One of the likeliest places in which to find Christ is in the garden of the Scriptures, for there He delights to walk. As of old, the blind men were wont to sit by the wayside begging, so that, if Jesus passed by, they might cry to Him; so would I have you sit down by the wayside of the Holy Scriptures. Hear the promises, listen to their gracious words. They are the footsteps of the Savior. As you hear them, may you be led to cry, "Thou Son of David, have mercy upon me!" Attend most those ministries which preach God's Word most. Do not select those that are fullest of fine speaking and that dazzle you with expressions which are rather ornamental than edifying. But get to a ministry that is full of God's own Word and, above all, learn God's Word itself. Read it with a desire to know its meaning, and I am persuaded that, thereby, many of you who are now far from God will be brought near to Him and led to a saving faith in Jesus, for "the word of the Lord is perfect, converting the soul." "Faith cometh by hearing, and hearing by the word of God."

The Word Is Personal

If the text says, "When thou awakest, it shall talk with thee," then it is clear the word is personal. "It shall talk with *thee*." Is it not written, "It shall speak to the air, and thou shalt hear its voice," but, "It shall talk with *thee*." You know exactly what the expression means. I am not exactly talking with any one of you this morning. There are too many of you, and I am but one. But, when you are on the road home, each one will talk with his fellow. Then it is truly talk when man speaks to man. Now, the Word of God has the condescending habit of talking to men, speaking personally to them. Herein, I desire to commend the Word of God to your love. Oh! that you might esteem it very precious for this reason!

"It shall talk *with thee*," that is to say, *God's word talks about men, and about modern men.* It speaks of ourselves and of these latter days as precisely as if it had only appeared this last week. Some go to the Word of God with the idea that they shall find historical information about the ancient ages, and so they will, but that is not the object of the Word. Others look for facts upon geology, and great attempts have been made either to bring geology around to Scripture or Scripture to geology. We may always rest assured that truth never contradicts itself. But, as nobody knows anything yet about geology—for its theory is a dream and an imagination altogether—we will wait until the philosophers settle their own private matters, being confident that when they find out the truth, it will be quite consistent with what God has revealed. At any rate, we may leave that. The main teachings of Holy Scripture are about men, about the Paradise of unfallen manhood, the fall, the degeneracy of the race, and the means of its redemption. The book speaks of victims and sacrifices, priests and washings, and so points us to the divine plan by which man can be elevated from the fall and be reconciled to God. Read Scripture through and you shall find that its great subject is that which concerns the race as to their most important interests, and concerns the race, not as Jews or as Gentiles, but as men; not as Barbarians, or Scythians, or Greek, or bond, or free, but as men. He does not read the Word of God aright who does not hear it talking to him about things which intimately concern both himself and his fellows. It is a book that talks, talks personally, for it deals with things not in the moon, nor in the planet Jupiter, nor in the distant ages long gone by, nor does it say much of the periods yet to come. But it deals with *us,* with the business of today, how sin may be today forgiven, and our souls brought at once into union with Christ.

Moreover, this book is so personal that *it speaks to men in all states and conditions before God.* How it talks to sinners—talks, I say, for it puts it thus: "Come, now, and let us reason together; though your sins be as scarlet, they shall be as wool; though they be red like crimson, they shall be as snow." It has many very tender expostulations for sinners. It stoops to their condition and position. If they will not stoop to God, it makes, as it were, eternal mercy stoop to them. It talks of feasts of fat things, of fat things full of marrow. The Book, as it talks, reasons with men's hunger and bids them eat and be satisfied. It speaks of garments woven in the loom of infinite wisdom and love, and so it talks to man's nakedness and entreats him to be arrayed in the divine righteousness. There is no sinner, in any condition, who dare say there is nothing in the Word of God to suit his case. If you have been a persecutor, Saul's history talks to you. If you had shed innocent blood very much, Manasseh would speak with you. If you have been a harlot or a thief, it has special passages to meet you. In all conditions into which the sinner can be cast, there is a word that precisely meets his condition.

And, certainly, when we become the children of God the book talks with us wondrously. In the family of heaven it is the child's own book. We no sooner know our Father than this dear book comes at once as a love letter from the far-off country, signed with our own Father's hand and perfumed with our Father's love. If we grow in grace, or if we backslide, in either case Scripture still talks with us. Whatever our position before the eternal God, the book seems to be written on purpose to meet that position. It talks to you as you are, not only as you should be, or as others have been, but with you, with you personally, about your present condition.

Have you never noticed how personal the book is as *to all your states of mind,* in reference to sadness or to joy? There was a time with some of us when we were very gloomy and sore depressed, and then the book of Job mourned to the same dolorous tune. I have turned over the Lamentations of Jeremiah and thought that I could have written what Jeremiah wrote. It mourns to us when we lament. On the other hand, when the soul gets up to the exceeding high mountains, to the top of Amana and Lebanon, when we behold visions of glory and see our Beloved face to face, lo! the Word is at our side. In the delightful language of the Psalms, or in the yet sweeter expressions of the Song of Solomon, it tells us all that is in our hearts. It talks to us as a living thing that has been in the deeps and has been on the heights, that has known the overwhelmings of affliction and has rejoiced in the triumphs of delight. The Word of God is to me my own book. I have no doubt, brother, it is the same to you. There could not be a Bible that suited me better. It seems written on purpose for me. Dear sister, have you not often felt as you have put your finger on a promise, "Ah, that is my promise. If there be no other soul whose tearful eyes can bedew that page and say, 'It is mine,' yet I, a poor afflicted one, can do so!" Oh, yes; the book is very personal, for it goes into all the details of our case, let our state be what it may.

And, *how very faithful it always is.* You never find the Word of God keeping back that which is profitable to you. Like Nathan it cries, "Thou art the man." It never allows our sins to go unrebuked, nor our backslidings to escape notice until they grow into overt sin. It gives us timely notice. It cries to us as soon as we begin to go aside, "Awake thou that sleepest," "Watch and pray," "Keep thine heart with all diligence," and a thousand other words of warning does it address personally to each one of us.

Now I would suggest, before I leave this point, a little self-examination as healthful for each of us. Does the Word of God after this fashion speak to my soul? Then it is a gross folly to lose by generalizations that precious thing which can only be realized by a personal grasp. How say you, dear hearer? Do you read the book for yourself and does the book speak to you? Has it ever condemned you, and have you trembled before the Word of God? Has it ever pointed you to Christ, and have you looked to Jesus the incarnate Savior? Does the book now seal, as with the witness of the Spirit, the witness of your own spirit that you are born of God? Are you in the habit of going to the Book to know your own condition, to see your own fate as in a glass? Is it your family medicine? Is it your test and tell-tale to let you know your spiritual condition? Oh, do not treat the Book otherwise than this, for if you do thus to it, and take it to be your personal friend, happy are you, since God will dwell with the man that trembles at His Word. But, if you treat it as anybody's book rather than your own, then beware, lest you be numbered with the wicked who despise God's statutes.

The Word Is Very Familiar

From the text we learn that Holy Scripture is very familiar. "When thou awakest, it shall *talk with* thee." To talk signifies fellowship, communion, familiarity. It does not say, "It shall preach to thee." Many persons have a high esteem for the Book, but they look upon it as though it were some very elevated teacher speaking to them from a lofty tribunal, while they stand far below. I will not altogether condemn that reverence, but it were far better if they would understand the familiarity of God's Word. It does not so much preach to us as *talk* to us. It is not, "When thou awakest, it shall lecture thee," or, "it shall scold thee." No, no, "it shall *talk* with thee." We sit at its feet, or rather at the feet of Jesus in the Word, and it comes down to us. It is familiar with us as a man talks to his friend. And here let me remind you of the delightful familiarity of Scripture in this respect that *it speaks the language of men.* If God had written us a book in His own language, we could not have comprehended it, or what little we understood would have so alarmed us that we should have besought that those words should not be spoken to us any more. But the Lord, in His Word, often uses language which, though it be infallibly true in its meaning, is not after the knowledge of God, but according to the manner of man. I mean this, that the Word uses similies and analogies of which we may say that they speak humanly, and not according to the absolute truth as God Himself sees it. As men conversing with babes use their broken speech, so does the condescending Word. It is not written in the celestial tongue, but in the *patois* of this lowland country, condescending to men of low estate. It feeds us on bread broken down to our capacity, "food convenient for us." It speaks of God's arm, His hand, His finger, His wings, and even of His feathers. Now, all this is familiar picturing, to meet our childish capacities; for the Infinite One is not to be conceived of as though such similitudes were literal facts. It is an amazing instance of divine love that He puts those things so that we may be helped to grasp sublime truths. Let us thank the Lord of the Word for this.

How tenderly Scripture *comes down to simplicity*. Suppose the sacred volume had all been like the book of the prophet Ezekiel, small would have been its service to the generality of mankind. Imagine that the entire volume had been as mysterious as the Book of Revelation. It might have been our duty to study it, but if its benefit depended upon our understanding it, we should have failed to attain it. But how simple are the gospels, how plain these words, "He that believeth and is baptized shall be saved." How deliciously clear those parables about the lost piece of money, the lost sheep, and the prodigal son. Wherever the word touches upon vital points, it is as bright as a sunbeam. Mysteries there are, and profound doctrines, deep where Leviathan can swim. But, where it has to do immediately with what concerns us for eternity, it is so plain that the babe in grace may safely wade in its refreshing streams. In the Gospel narrative the wayfaring man, though a fool, need not err. It is familiar talk; it is God's great mind bought down to our littleness that it may lift us up.

How familiar the book is too—I speak now as to my own feelings— *as to all that concerns us*. It talks about my flesh and my corruptions and my sins as only one that knew me could speak. It talks of my trials in the wisest way. Some, I dare not tell, it knows all about. It talks about my difficulties. Some would sneer at them and laugh, but this Book sympathizes with them, knows my tremblings, my fears, my doubts, and all the storm that rages within the little world of my nature. The book has been through all my experience. Somehow or other it maps it all out and talks with me as if it were a fellow-pilgrim. It does not speak to me unpractically, and scold me, and look down upon me from an awful height of stern perfection, as if it were an angel and could not sympathize with fallen men. But like the Lord whom it reveals, the Book seems as if it were touched with a feeling of my infirmities and had been tempted in all points as I am. Have you not often wondered at the human utterances of the divine Word. It thunders like

God and yet weeps like man. It seems impossible that anything should be too little for the Word of God to notice, or too bitter, or even too sinful for that Book to overlook. It touches humanity at all points. Everywhere it is a personal, familiar acquaintance, and scorns to say to itself, "Shall I hide this thing from Abraham my friend?"

And, how often the book has *answered inquiries!* I have been amazed in times of difficulties to see how plain the oracle is. You have asked friends, and they could not advise you; but you have gone to your knees, and God has told you. You have questioned, and you have puzzled, and you have tried to elucidate the problem, and, lo! in the chapter read at morning prayer or in a passage of Scripture that lay open before you, the direction has been given. Have we not seen a text, as it were, plume its wings and fly from the word like a seraph, and touch our lips with a live altar coal? It lay like a slumbering angel amidst the beds of spices of the sacred Word, but it received a divine mission, and brought consolation and instruction to your heart.

The Word of God, then, talks with us in the sense of being familiar with us. Do we understand this? I will close this point by another word of application. Who, then, that finds God's Word so dear and kind a friend would spurn or neglect it? If any of you have despised it, what shall I say to you? If it were a dreary book, written within and without with curses and lamentations, whose every letter flashed with declarations of vengeance, I might see some reason why we should not read it. But, O precious, priceless companion, dear friend of all my sorrows, making my bed in my sickness, the light of my darkness, and the joy of my soul, how can I forget you—how can I forsake you? I have heard of one who said that the dust on some men's Bibles lay there so thick and long that you might write *"Damnation"* on it. I am afraid that such is the case with some of you. Mr. Rogers of Dedham on one occasion, after preaching about the preciousness of the Bible, took it away from the front of the pulpit, and, putting it down behind him, pictured God as saying, "You do not read the book. You do not care about it. I will take it back—you shall not be wearied with it any more." And then he portrayed the grief of wise men's hearts when they found the blessed revelation withdrawn from men. How they would besiege the throne of grace, day and night, to ask it back. I am sure he spoke the truth. Though we too much neglect it, yet ought we to prize it beyond all price, for, if it were taken from us, we should have lost our kindest comforter in the hour of need. God grant us to love the Scriptures more!

The Word Is Responsive

Fourthly, and with brevity, our text evidently shows that the Word is responsive. "When thou awakest, it shall talk *with* thee," not *to* you.

Now, talk with a man is not all on one side. To talk with a man needs answering talk from him. You have both of you something to say when you talk together. It is a conversation to which each one contributes his part. Now, Scripture is a marvelously conversational Book; it talks, and makes men talk. It is ever ready to respond to us. Suppose you go to the Scriptures in a certain state of spiritual life. You must have noticed, I think, that the Word answers to that state. If you are dark and gloomy, it will appear as though it had put itself in mourning, so that it might lament with you. When you are on the dunghill, there sits Scripture with dust and ashes on its head, weeping side by side with you, and not upbraiding like Job's miserable comforters. But suppose you come to the Book with gleaming eyes of joy, you will hear it laugh. It will sing and play to you as with psaltery and harp, it will bring forth the high-sounding cymbals. Enter its goodly land in a happy state, and you shall go forth with joy and be led forth with peace, its mountains and its hills shall break before you into singing, and all the trees of the field shall clap their hands. As in water the face is reflected, so in the living stream of revealed truth a man sees his own image.

If you come to Holy Scripture with growth in grace and with aspirations for yet higher attainments, the Book grows with you, grows upon you. It is ever beyond you and cheerily cries, "Higher yet; Excelsior!" Many books in my library are now behind and beneath me. I read them years ago with considerable pleasure. I have read them since with disappointment. I shall never read them again for they are of no service to me. They were good in their way once, and so were the clothes I wore when I was ten years old. But I outgrew them, I know more than those books know, and know wherein they are faulty. Nobody ever outgrows Scripture. The Book widens and deepens with our years. It is true, it cannot really grow for it is perfect. But it does so to our apprehension. The deeper you dig into Scripture, the more you find that it is a great abyss of truth. The beginner learns four or five points of orthodoxy and says, "I understand the Gospel. I have grasped all the Bible." Wait a bit, and when his soul grows and knows more of Christ, he will confess, "Thy commandment is exceeding broad, I have only begun to understand it."

There is one thing about God's Word which shows its responsiveness to us, and that is when you reveal your heart to it, it reveals its heart to you. If, as you read the Word, you say, "O blessed truth, you are indeed realized in my experience, come still further into my heart. I give up my prejudices, I assign myself, like the wax, to be stamped with your seal"—when you do that and open your heart to Scripture, Scripture will open its heart to you for it has secrets which it does not tell to the eternal reader. It has precious things of the everlasting hills which can only be discovered by miners who know how to dig and open the secret places, and penetrate great veins of everlasting riches. Give yourself up to the Bible, and the Bible will give itself up to you. Be candid with it and honest with your soul, and the Scripture will take down its golden key and open one door after another. It will show to your astonished gaze ingots of silver which you could not weigh and heaps of gold which you could not measure. Happy is that man who, in talking with the Bible, tells it all his heart and learns the secret of the Lord which is with them that fear Him.

And how, too, if you love the Bible and talk out your love to it, the Bible will love you! Its wisdom says, "I love them that love me." Embrace the Word of God, and the Word of God embraces you at once. When you prize its every letter, then it smiles upon you graciously, greets you with many welcomes, and treats you as an honored guest. I am always sorry to be on bad terms with the Bible, for then I must be on bad terms with God. Whenever my creed does not square with God's Word, I think it is time to mold my creed into another form. As for God's words, they must not be touched with hammer or ax. Oh, the chiseling, and cutting, and hammering in certain commentaries to make God's Bible orthodox and systematic! How much better to leave it alone! The Word is right, and we are wrong, wherein we agree not with it. The teachings of God's Word are infallible and must be reverenced as such. Now, when you love it so well that you would not touch a single line of it, and prize it so much that you would even die for the defense of one of its truths, then, as it is dear to you, you will be dear to it. It will grasp you and unfold itself to you as it does not to the world.

Dear brethren and sisters, I must leave this point, but it shall be with this remark—Do you talk to God? Does God talk to you? Does your heart go up to heaven, and does His Word come fresh from heaven to your soul? If not, you do not know the experience of the living child of God, and I can earnestly pray you may. May you this day be brought to see Christ Jesus in the Word, to see a crucified Savior there and to put your trust in Him. Then, from this day forward, the Word will echo to your heart—it will respond to your emotions.

The Word Is Influential

Lastly, Scripture is influential. That I gather from the fact that Solomon says, "When thou wakest, it shall talk with thee." Solomon then follows it up with the remark that it keeps man from the strange woman and from other sins which he goes on to mention. When the Word of God talks with us, it influences us. All talk influences more or less. I believe there is more done in this world for good or bad by talk than there is by preaching; indeed, the preacher preaches best when he talks. There is no oratory in the world that is equal to simple talk. It is the model of eloquence, and all your rhetorician's action and verbiage are so much rubbish. The most efficient way of preaching is simply talking—the man permitting his heart to run over at his lips into other men's hearts. Now, this Book, as it talks with us, influences us, and it does so in many ways.

It soothes our sorrows and encourages us. Many a warrior has been ready to steal away from God's battle, but the Word has laid its hand on him and said, "Stand on thy feet, be not discouraged, be of good cheer, I will strengthen thee, I will help thee; yea, I will uphold thee with the right hand of my righteousness." Brave saints we have read of, but we little know how often they would have been arrant cowards, only the good Word came and strengthened them. Then they went back to be stronger than lions and swifter than eagles.

While the book thus soothes and cheers, it has a wonderfully elevating power. Have you never felt it put fresh life-blood into you? You have thought, "How can I continue to live at such a dying rate as I have lived, something nobler must I gain?" Read that part of the Word which tells of the agonies of your Master, and you will feel—

> Now for the love I bear his name,
> What was my gain I count my loss
> My former pride I call my shame,
> And nail my glory to his cross.

Read of the glories of heaven which this book reveals, and you will feel that you can run the race with quickened speed, because a crown so bright is glittering in your view. Nothing can so lift a man above the gross considerations of carnal gain or human applause as to have his soul saturated with the spirit of truth. It elevates as well as cheers.

Then, too, how often it warns and restrains. I had gone to the right or to the left if the law of the Lord had not said, "Let thine eyes look right on, and let thine eyelids look straight before thee."

This Book's consecrated talk sanctifies and molds the mind into the image of Christ. You cannot expect to grow in grace if you do not read the Scriptures. If you are not familiar with the Word, you cannot expect to become like Him that spoke it. Our experience is, as it were, the potter's wheel on which we revolve. The hand of God is in the Scriptures to mold us after the fashion and image which He intends to bring us to. Oh, be much with the Holy Word of God and you will be holy. Be much with the silly novels of the day and the foolish trifles of the hour, and you will degenerate into vapid wasters of your time. But be much with the solid teaching of God's Word, and you will become solid and substantial men and women. Drink them in and feed upon them, and they shall produce in you a Christlikeness at which the world shall stand astonished.

Lastly, let the Scripture talk with you, and it will confirm and settle you. We hear every now and then of apostates from the Gospel. They must have been little taught in the truth as it is in Jesus. A great outcry is made, every now and then, about our all being perverted to Rome. I was assured the other day by a good man, with a great deal of alarm, that all England was going over to Popery. I told him I did not know what kind of God he worshiped, but my God was a good deal bigger than the Devil and did not intend to let the Devil have his way after all. And I told him that I was not half as much afraid of the Pope at Rome as the Ritualists at home. But mark it, there is some truth in these fears. There will be a going over to one form of error or another, unless there be in the Christian church a more honest, industrious, and general reading of Holy Scripture. What if I were to say most of you church members do not read your Bibles, would I be slandering you? You hear on Sunday a chapter read and you perhaps read a passage at family prayer, but a very large number never read the Bible privately for themselves. They take their religion out of the monthly magazine or accept it from the minister's lips. Oh, for the Berean spirit back again, to search the Scriptures whether these things be so. I would like to see a huge pile of all the books, good and bad that were ever written—prayer books, sermons, hymn books, and all—smoking like Sodom of old if the reading of those books keeps you away from the reading of the Bible. For a ton weight of human literature is not worth an ounce of Scripture. One single drop of the essential tincture of the Word of God is better than a sea full of our commentings and sermonizings, and the like. The Word, the simple, pure, infallible Word of God, we must live upon if we are to become strong against error and tenacious of truth. Friends, may you be established in the faith, rooted, grounded, built up. But I know you cannot be except you search the Scriptures continually.

The time is coming when we shall all fall asleep in death. Oh, how blessed it will be to find when we awake that the Word of God will talk with us then and remember its ancient friendship. Then the promise which we loved before shall be fulfilled. The charming intimations of a blessed future shall be all realized. The face of Christ, whom we saw as through a glass darkly, shall be all uncovered, and He shall shine upon us as the sun in its strength. God grant us to love the Word and feed thereon, and the Lord shall have the glory forever and ever. Amen and amen.

3

The Waterer Watered

He that watereth shall be watered also himself (Proverbs 11:25).

The general principle is that in living for the good of others we shall be profited also ourselves. We must not isolate our own interests but feel that we live for others. This teaching is sustained by the analogy of nature, for in nature there is a law that no one thing can be independent of the rest of creation, but there is a mutual action and reaction of all upon all. All the constituent parts of the universe are bound to one another by invisible chains, and there is not a single creature in it which springs up, flourishes, or decays for itself alone. The very planets, though they float far from one another, exercise attraction. The fixed stars, though they seem to be infinitely remote, are still linked to one another by mysterious bonds. God has so constituted this universe, that selfishness is the greatest possible offense against His law. Living for others and ministering to others is the strictest obedience to His will. Our surest road to our own happiness is to seek the good of our fellows. We store up in God's own bank what we generously expend on the behalf of our race. The little spring bubbling forth from the ancient pipe on the hillside overflows the stone basin and liberally supplies all the villagers with pure and cooling drink. In its flowing it does not waste itself, for the deep fountains in the bowels of the earth continue unceasingly to supply it, and both in winter's frost and summer's drought, the springhead yields its crystal stream. The little brook which babbles through the wood, hiding among stones, leaping down the moss-grown rocks, and anon deepening and swelling its stream, pours all its gatherings into the river, hoarding not a drop. Though its treasure is constantly being lavished with unstinting liberality, yet heaven and earth see to it that the brook shall never fail to sing its joyous song,

---

This sermon was taken from *The Metropolitan Tabernacle Pulpit* and was preached on Sunday morning, April 23, 1865.

Men may come and go,
But I go on forever.

The river hastens with its greater floods toward the all-receiving
ocean, pouring itself out every hour with happy plenteousness, as
though it only existed to empty itself. Yet the abundant tributaries
which come streaming from the hills and draining the valleys are careful that the river shall know no lack, but shall be kept constantly brim-
ming a joyous and bounding river evermore. The ocean perpetually
sends up its steaming exhalations to the sky, grudging nothing. It puts
no doors to its rolling waves, but uncovers all its treasure to the sun,
and the sun makes large draughts upon the royal exchequer of the deep.
Nevertheless the ocean is not diminished, for all the rivers are constantly conspiring to keep the sea full to the shore. The clouds of
heaven, when they are full of rain, empty themselves upon the earth.
Yet the clouds cease not to be, for "they return after the rain," and the
ocean down below seems but to be too glad to be continually feeding its
sister ocean on the other side of the firmament. So, as wheels with
bands are made to work together, as wheels with cogs working upon
one another, the whole watery machinery is kept in motion by each part
acting upon its next neighbor, and the next upon the next. Each wheel
expends its force upon its fellow, and the whole find a recompense in
their mutual action upon one another.

The same truth might be illustrated from other departments of nature. If we view this microcosm, the human body, we shall find that the
heart does not receive the blood to store it up, but while it pumps it in at
one valve, it sends it forth at another. The blood is always circulating
everywhere and is stagnant nowhere. The same is true of all the fluids
in a healthy body, they are in a constant state of expenditure. If one cell
stores for a few moments its peculiar secretion, it only retains it until it
is perfectly fitted for its appointed use in the body. For if any cell in the
body should begin to store up its secretion, its store would soon become
the cause of inveterate disease. No, the organ would soon lose the
power to secrete at all if it did not give forth its products. The whole of
the human system lives by giving. The eye cannot say to the foot, I
have no need of you and will not guide you. For if it does not perform
its watchful office, the whole man will be in the ditch, and the eye will
be covered with mire. If the members refuse to contribute to the general
stock, the whole body will become poverty-stricken and be given up to
the bankruptcy of death. Let us learn, then, from the analogy of nature
the great lesson—that to get, we must give; that to accumulate, we must
scatter; that to make ourselves happy, we must make others happy; and
that to get good and become spiritually vigorous, we must do good and
seek the spiritual good of others. This is the general principle.

The text suggests a particular personal application of the general principle. We shall consider it, first, *in its narrowest sense, as belonging to ourselves personally;* secondly, *in a wider sense, as it may refer to us as a church;* then, thirdly, *in its widest sense, as it may be referred to the entire body of Christ,* showing that still it is true that as it waters, so it shall be watered itself.

In Reference to Ourselves Personally

There are some works in which we cannot all engage. Peculiar men are called to be God's great woodsmen, to clear the way with the ax, to go before His army like our sappers and miners—such men as Martin Luther, Calvin, and Zwingle—that glorious trio of heroes marching in front of reformation and evangelization. They are cutting down the tall trees, tunneling the hills, and bridging the rivers. We smaller men feel that there is little of this work for us to do. But when the backwoodsmen have cleared the forest, after all the roots are grubbed, and the soil is burned and plowed, then comes the sowing and the planting. In this all the household can take a place. When the plants have sprung up and need water, it is not only the stalwart man with the ax who can now apply himself to watering, but even the little children can take a share in this lighter work. Watering is work for persons of all grades and all sorts. If I cannot carry about me some ponderous load as the Eastern water-bearer can, yet I will take my little water pot, my little jug or pitcher, and go to the well. For if I cannot water the forest tree, I may water the tiny plant which grows at its root. Watering is work for all sorts of people. So then we will make a personal application to every Christian here this morning: you can all do something in watering, and this promise can therefore be realized by all of you, "He that watereth shall be watered also himself."

All God's plants, more or less, want watering. You and I do. We cannot live long without fresh supplies of grace. Hence the value of the promise, "I, the Lord, do keep it; I will water it every moment." There are no rills at our root as we grow in the soil of nature. It is only in the garden of grace that we are "like trees planted by the rivers of water, bringing forth our fruit in our season." If the Lord Jesus who is the stem of the vine should cease to supply us with the fresh sap of grace, would we not be like the withered branch which is cast over the wall to be burned in the fire?

The Lord's people usually get this watering through instrumentality. God does not speak to us out of heaven with His own voice—perhaps the thunder might appall us. He does not write texts of Scripture with His own finger in letters of fire across the sky, but he waters us by instrumentality, by His Word written and His Word preached, or otherwise uttered by His servants. His Holy Spirit waters us by the admonitions of parents, by the kind suggestions of friends, by the teaching of His ministers, by the example of all His saints. The Holy Spirit waters us, but He takes care to do it by our fellow-workers, putting an honor upon His own servants by using them in instrumentality.

This being fully believed by us all, we may proceed to another truth, namely, that *some of His servants especially want watering* and should therefore be the objects of our constant care. Some plants need watering from their peculiar *nature*. A gardener will tell you that certain flowers require very little water, perhaps for months they will grow in a stony soil. But others must be watered regularly and plenteously or they will soon droop. Some of you, my dear brothers and sisters, are so desponding that if you did not receive much comfort you would hardly hold up your heads at all. You are so weak in the faith that if you were not fed with milk continually you would scarcely be alive. "Comfort ye, comfort ye, my people, saith your God"—is especially applicable to the mourners in Zion. Their constitutional temperament is such, that to maintain the lamp of their joy they require much oil of comfort. Perhaps, too, they are ignorant, and the *ignorant* want much watering. If they knew the doctrines of grace more fully, they might go to the wells themselves. But not knowing where the water is, or feeling like the woman at the well that the well is deep and that there is nothing to draw with, they cannot get the water. We who are instructed in the way of God must take care that we bring up the water for them with our longer length of the line of knowledge, so that they may not fail to be watered.

It may be, the need is not so much caused by the nature of the plant, but by *the position in which it is placed*. Many of you are very happily situated where you can constantly attend the means of grace, where the family altar smokes with sweet perfume, where you cannot well help growing, for you are like plants in a hothouse. But there are others on the contrary who live in houses were *the jeer* is far more frequently heard than the voice of praise; where, instead of being helped in your devotions, you are hindered. Your spirit is driven to and fro with distractions. From the very closet where you wanted to commune with God, you are forced out by cruel mocking. We ought to be very tender over your condition, as being planted on no fruitful hill, but on a very thirsty land where no water is. Your position should lead God's people to watch you with deepest interest, and see to it that you are well watered.

I may mention also *the sick*. When our dear friends are tried with bodily pain, when they are shut up week after week from the public gatherings, then they want watering. Their position is such that we ought to be specially mindful of them. It is written, "He carrieth the lambs in his bosom and gently leads those that are with young." We must note the peculiar condition of the saints of God, being most careful of those who most need our tenderness.

Let me also suggest *the young* to you. These want watering, both, let me say, from their character and from their position. With little experience and little knowledge, they are prone to wander or to be seized by the wolf. Tend them with parental affection. When slips of flowers are first put into the ground, they want more water than they will afterward. When they have sent out more roots, and these roots have abundant fibers searching through the soil for moisture, they may not require much of the gardener's care, but just now they must have it or die. Therefore, I say, let the feeble, the weak, the young, the sick, the persecuted, be watered most anxiously and lovingly by you all.

Certain dear friends need watering, not so much from their position and character, as from *the present trials through which they are passing*. Certain plants after long standing in the sun droop their leaves and look as if they must wither and die. But as soon as water is poured to their roots, it has sometimes perfectly surprised me to see how they will recover. I could scarcely think that they were the same plants, their recovery was so sudden. The little roots beneath sent the message up to the main roots and said, "We have found out moisture. A friendly hand has given us a supply." The root talked to the stem, and the stem rejoiced. The great leaves drank up their share, and the little leaves sucked up their drops, until the whole plant to the very summit was verdant once more and rejoiced. Times will come to all of us when we want water. I, myself, get very desponding at seasons, and I suppose you do. Unbelief dries us up. Oh that devil of unbelief! Why, if that demon were dead, the other devil we might very well contend with. Personal affliction, losses, crosses, burdens, make us just like the withering shrub, and then we want to have the consolations of some kind friend to water us.

Dear friends, sometimes there are those in the church who particularly want watering because they are *actually withering*. It is not to maintain verdure in their case but to restore it. Those backsliding ones, those who have slipped with their feet, do not cast them off, for God casts not off the backsliding one. When they begin to forsake the house of God, do not forsake *them*. Follow them with your tears. In such a church as this, if you do not exercise mutual oversight over one another, we shall simply become a mass of corruption instead of being a mountain of holiness. Watch over your fellow Christians as soon as you see the first signs of declension. When they forsake the prayer meetings, gently give them a hint of the evil of lukewarmness, and the danger of falling little by little. When you mark the first sign in their outward carriage of laxity with regard to divine things, when you see coldness where there was formerly zeal, be sure to give a gentle word of earnest, pathetic admonition. As I look around this Tabernacle, I can but compare these rising seats to shelves in the conservatory. You are the plants which must all be watered, or you will languish and wither. I, who have to be my Master's undergardener, am very anxious to say to all of you who have any water in your watering-pots, help me to water these plants, that, by the gracious operations of God the Holy Spirit, they may be kept fruitful, green, verdant in spiritual things even to the end.

We now enter more thoroughly into our text, and observe that *all believers have power to water others.* You may not have much ability or influence, but you all have some power in this matter. In thinking over what Solomon meant, it struck me that he had in his mind's eye the plan of irrigation which is followed in some Eastern countries. The rivers at certain seasons overflow their banks. The careful husbandmen whose farms are close along the sides of the bank have large tanks and reservoirs in which they store up the water. After the flood the river is comparatively empty, and the little farms, the vineyards, and pastures on the banks begin to cry out for water. Then the careful husbandman lets out the water from his tank or reservoir by slow degrees and uses it with great economy. It would sometimes happen that one of these farmers would have his reservoirs filled, and his next neighbor, perhaps through the bursting of a tank or the falling down of the bank of earth, might have little or no water. At such times a churlish man would say, "I shall want all my water for myself, I will not lend or give so much as a drop of it. I have none to spare." But the generous man says, "I do not know whether God may be pleased to send a drought or not, but I cannot let my neighbor lose all his crops for the wait of a little water while I have a good stock in hand." So he pulls up the sluice, and lets such a stream as he thinks he can spare flow into his neighbor's channel, that he may water his fields therewith. Now Solomon says that those who water others shall be watered. Hence, next season it may happen that this good man may have no water himself. Well, then, all the farmers around about will say, "Why, he helped us when his tank was full, and we will return his kindness into his bosom." "Ah," says one, "he saved me from ruin. I should not have had a crop at all last season if it had not been for him." So they all lend a portion, until he finds no difficulty whatever. Even in a season of drought, when men cannot get water for love or money, he is sure to have it. The common feeling of men, as a usual rule, recognizes the law of gratitude. Men say, "He watered others, he shall be watered himself." My dear brother, you may be a man of talent, you may be a man of wealth, just turn on the big tap, and let your ignorant or poor neighbors benefit a little by your abundance. Pull up the floodgates, and let the more needy ones be enriched by your fullness. Open that mouth of yours that your wisdom may feed many. Tell of what God has done for your soul that the humble may hear thereof and be glad. Do not be a reservoir brimmed up until the banks are ready to burst out through the weight which presses upon them, but just let some of the treasure run out. When *your* time of need shall come—and who knows when it may overtake any of us?—you shall find willing friends who shall run with swift feet to cheer your adversity.

This simile needs to be supplemented by another: many true saints are unable to do much. See, then, the gardeners going down to the pond and dipping in their watering pots to carry the refreshing liquid to the flowers. A child comes into the garden and wishes to help. Yonder is a little watering pot for him. Now, see that little water pot, though it does not carry so much, yet it carries the same water. It does not make any difference to the half-dozen flowers which get that water whether it came out of the big pot or the little pot, so long as it is the same water and they get it. You who are like children in God's church, you who do not know much, yet try and tell to others what you do know. If it be the same Gospel truth and it be blessed by the same Spirit, it will not matter to the souls who get blessed by you whether they were blessed by a man or woman of one or ten talents. What difference will it make to me whether I was converted to God by means of a poor woman who was never made a blessing to anybody else or by one who had brought his thousands to the Savior's feet? Go, my dear friends, and exercise the holy art of watering. You say "How?" Why, a word may do it, a look may do it, an action may do it. Only zealously desire to offer sympathy, to afford instruction, to give needed help, to impart what you may be favored with to others, and you shall be watering yourselves.

The main point is, that *in so watering others we shall be watered ourselves.* I am sure we shall, for God promises it and He always keeps His promise. If I want to get water I must give water. Though that seems a strange way of self-serving I pray you try it. Was not that a very singular thing that when the poor woman of Sarepta had nearly exhausted all her meal, the prophet asked for a cake for himself. She had been very saving of it. I dare say she had eaten only a mouthful or two every day. She and her poor boy were looking very thin. They had come to the last handful. She thought, "I will make one cake for my son and myself, and then we will die." She is outside picking up sticks that she may bake this cake. God intends to bless her. How does He do it? There comes His prophet, the hairy man, and the first word he says to her is, "Fetch me, I pray thee, a little water in a vessel, that I may drink." She is quite ready to serve anyone and away she hastens for the water, when Elijah cries aloud, "Bring me, I pray thee, a morsel of bread in thine hand." What, out of that little handful—only enough for one? "Yes," he says, "make me thereof a little cake first, and after make for thee and thy son." "After that!" she might have said, "what will be left after that? When there is only a handful of meal and a little oil in a cruse, not enough for one, am I to give that to you and *afterward* see to myself and child?" Faith enabled her to obey, and from that very moment neither she nor her son ever knew what want was. She gave from her little, and her little multiplied. The case of the woman of Zarephath is but one of thousands establishing the rule of God's mode of action with his church, a rule which shall not be broken until time shall end.

Let me show you how you will get watered yourself. In the first place, if you try to do good to others it will do you good by *waking up your powers*. Thousands of men do not know what they are made of. You have no idea what a fine fellow you are, young man, until you begin to shake yourself a little and go forth to fight the Lord's battles. We do not know what sinews we have until we climb the mountains. We do not know what strength there may be in our backs and arms until we have to carry a ponderous load, and then we find it out. You have latent talents, dormant faculties, which would work wonders if you could call them forth. Some people are not awake more than skin deep. All underneath the skin is sound asleep. They are like the great candle which I showed you one night with a small wick, which was only melted a little in the middle while all the outside was still cold, hard tallow, and did not contribute to the light. You have not become warm through yet, your whole souls have not been wound up to the right pitch for serving God. You have only a little earnestness, a little zeal. But if you ventured upon holy enterprises, you would bestir yourself so thoroughly that you would scarcely know yourself again. That would be a blessing indeed.

But next, *you would often find that in trying to water others you gained instruction.* Go talk to some poor saint to comfort her, and she will tell you what will comfort you. Oh, what gracious lessons some of us have learned at sickbeds! We went to teach the Scriptures, we came away blushing that we knew so little of them. We went to talk experimental truth, and we found we were only up to the ankles while here were God's poor saints breast-deep in the river of divine love. We learn by teaching, and our pupils often teach us.

You will also *get comfort in your work*. Rest assured that working for others is very happy exercise. Like the two men in the snow: one chafed the other's limbs to keep him from dying. In so doing, he kept his own blood in circulation, and his own life was preserved. Comfort God's people and the comfort will return into your own soul.

Watering others will make you *humble.* You will find better people in the world than yourself. You will be astonished to find how much grace there is where you thought there was none, and how much knowledge some have gained while you, as yet, have made little progress with far greater opportunities.

You will also *win many prayers.* Those who work for others get prayed for, and that is a swift way of growing rich in grace. Let me have your prayers, and I can do anything! Let me be without my people's prayers, and I can do nothing. You Sunday school teachers, if you are blessed to the conversion of the children, will get your children's prayers. You that conduct the larger classes in the conversion of your young people will be sure to have a wealth of love come back into your own bosoms, swimming upon the stream of supplication. You will thus be a blessing to yourselves.

In watering others you will *get honor to yourselves*, and that will help to water you by stimulating your future exertions. The Romans appointed censors in their State, not only to censure men for gross immoralities, but to require every man to give an account of what he was doing for the good of the Republic. We have deacons and elders— would it not be an additional blessing to have censors in the church to go around and ask the members, all of them, what they are doing for the good of the Christian church? A Greek historian desired very intensely to say a word about the people of the city where he was born. He felt he could not write his history without saying something of his own native place, and accordingly he wrote this, "While Athens was building temples, and Sparta was waging war, my countrymen were doing nothing." I am afraid there are too many Christians, of whom, if the book were written as to what they are doing in the church, it would have to be said they have been doing nothing all their lives. You would be delivered from that reproach if you began to water others.

Let me cease from this subject by saying, *while you are watering others, you will be manifesting and showing your love to Christ. That will make you more like Him,* and so you will be watered while you are seeking to benefit your neighbors. To serve Jesus! What need I say of that? Look into that face, bedewed with bloody sweat for you, and can you not sweat for Him? Look to those hands, pierced for you, and shall your hands hang idly down and not be used for Him? Look at those feet, fastened to the wood with nails for you! Can I ask of you any pilgrimage too long to repay the toil which those feet endured for your sake? My brethren and sisters, remember what Christ Jesus has done for you, from whence He came, the riches which He left, to what He came, the poverty and shame which He endured, and how He went down into the depths that He might take us up to the heights. If you will think of these, you will have the best motive, I think, for beginning to look after His lambs and fighting with those lions which seek to devour His flock. In that moving motive will be the main means by which you shall be conformed to His image, and shall become like Him, self-sacrificing, doing your Father's business.

I wish I could speak more powerfully this morning, but the matter ought to speak for itself with Christians. If we love Jesus, we shall not want any pleading with to water His plants. If you really love Him, it will not be a question of whether you shall do something, the only question will be, "What can I do?" You will say in your pew this morning, "What shall I render to the Lord for all His benefits toward me?" He has spared your lives. He has given you health and strength, provided you with spirituals and temporals. He has made your heart leap for joy at the sound of His name. He has plucked you out of the horrible pit and out of the miry clay. He has taken you out of the black bondage of the prince of darkness, and made you His sons and daughters. He has put the ring of His eternal love upon your finger, your feet are shod with the preparation of the Gospel of peace.

> This world is yours, and worlds to come,
> Earth is your lodge, and heaven your home.

There is a crown for your head, a palm branch for your hand, pavements of gold for your feet, and felicities forever for your entire soul. Even your body is to be raised again from the dust and fashioned like to Christ's glorious body. "Eye hath not seen, nor ear heard, neither have entered into the heart of man, the things which God hath prepared for you." Now what will you do for Him? Will you not win the promise that your soul shall be watered by seeking to water the souls of others?

A Brief Exhortation

This general principle is worthy of a wider application. We, as a church, dear friends, have enjoyed singular prosperity. While many churches have been depressed and decreased in numbers, we have increased. While other churches have had the hectic flush of a spurious revival, we have had one perpetual revival, lasting for nearly twelve years. I do not know that we have increased at a more or a less rapid rate. We could not increase more quickly, for we have not officers enough or time enough to see the converts as it is. We have never, I think, increased less, for the work seems to have ever the same prosperity about it. I praise God that I can say of my ministry in this place and elsewhere, that to this day it has the dew of its youth upon it. There are as many rejoicing to find Christ through the agencies employed in this church today as in the first day when we came among you in the freshness and vigor of our youth. We have had no schism. We have had no division. We have not been vexed with heresy. We have been blessed with something like persecution, but this has only bound us the faster to one another until we are like a threefold cord which cannot be broken. Like iron bars made red hot in the furnace and hammered together, we are not soon to be sundered from one another.

Now, dear friends, up to this time the policy which we have pursued has been this: if members of other churches want to know, we hereby tell them, *we have endeavored to water others.* Your minister has journeyed all over the three kingdoms preaching the Word, and you have not grumbled at his absence. We have undertaken many enterprises for Christ. We hope to undertake a great many more. We have never husbanded our strength. We have undertaken enterprises that were enough to exhaust us to which we became accustomed in due season, and then we have gone on to something more. We have never sought to hinder the uprising of other churches from our midst or in our neighborhood. It is with cheerfulness that we dismiss our twelves, our twenties, our fifties to form other churches. We encourage our members to leave us to found other churches. No, we seek to persuade them to do it. We ask them to scatter throughout the land, to become the goodly seed which God shall bless. I believe that so long as we do this, we shall prosper.

I have marked other churches that have adopted the other way, and they have not succeeded. This is what I have heard from some ministers: "I do not encourage village stations. Or, if I do, I do not encourage their becoming distinct churches and breaking bread together. I do not encourage too many young men going out to preach, for to have a knot of people who can preach a little may very soon cause dissatisfaction with my own preaching." I have marked those who have followed this course, and I have seen that the effect of trying to keep all the blood in the heart is to bring on congestion, and very soon the whole body has been out of health. My friends, if you can do more good elsewhere than you can do here, for God's sake, go and happy shall I be that you have gone. If you can serve my Master in the little rooms in the neighborhood, if by forming yourselves into smaller churches you can increase the honor of my Master's name, I shall love you nonetheless for going. But I shall delight to think that you have Christ's spirit in you, and can do and dare for His name's sake.

At the present moment we rejoice to know that many a Sunday school in this neighborhood is indebted to the members of this church for teachers. It is right. We do not want you at home, and are therefore glad to see you at work elsewhere. No matter, so long as Christ is preached whether you throw your strength into that church or into this church. Here, as being members with us, we have the first claim upon you. But when we do not need you by reason of our abundance of men, go and give your strength to any other part of Christ's church that may desire you.

While I speak thus much in your praise, my brethren and sisters, let me say, we must keep this up. If we say, "We have the college to support. We do as much as other churches for various societies and can be content to sit still," this church will begin to go rotten at the core the moment we are not working for God with might and main. Sometimes I get a pull at my coattail by very kind, judicious friends, who think I shall ask you to do too much. You are welcome to pull my coattail, but it will come off before I shall stand back for a moment. As long as I live I must serve my Master with my whole soul. When you think I go too fast, you can stand back *if you dare*, for mark, you will be responsible to God if you do. You may start back if you will, and if you dare, but I must go on, *must* go on, MUST go on, or else I die. You that are worthy of the day in which you live will follow me, step by step, in any good project. Though I should seem too rash, you will redeem me from the charge of rashness by the enthusiasm and the earnestness with which you carry out my plans.

Here is this great city! Was there ever such spiritual destitution? A million people who could not go to a place of worship if they had the heart to go there! And here we have the priestcraft of the Church of England increasing the spiritual destitution by building fresh churches. Not providing for it, but increasing it I say, for I reckon that wherever Puseyism is preached, there is an increase of spiritual destitution. Wherever broad churchism comes, there is an increase of spiritual destitution. It is little better where they go who preach the Gospel in the pulpit, and read popery at the font, the grave, and the bedside. In this last case public morality is shocked by the perjury of those who swear to a prayer book in which they do not believe. Much as I respect and even love believers in the Anglican establishment, I can only feel that their presence in so corrupt a body is the reason why it exists. I therefore think them to be doing mischief by buttressing a falling and ruinous cause.

True Protestants, we must take upon ourselves to work for London as if there were no other agencies at work except those of the free churches. For the Hagar Church, the church which has a mortal for its head; the harlot church which lives in alliance with the State, has too many sins of her own to repent of to be of much use in this hour of peril. The good she can do is so insignificant that it is not worthwhile to compute it because the monstrous evil which she fosters and perpetrates is a more than sufficient set-off against it. *We* must work and toil and labor to scatter in every lane, alley, and court of London the pure

Gospel of the blessed God. Let people know that Sacramentarianism is a lie, that there is no salvation but in the uplifted Cross of Christ, and no salvation through ceremonies but only through a simple faith in Him who loved us and gave Himself for us. If you among others are come to the kingdom for such a time as this, it shall be well with you. But if not, you shall be put away as things abhorred, and this place shall be a hissing and a byword in generations yet to come. It shall be said of you, there lived a people who were led by a man, who, with all his faults, was in earnest and was honest. They would not follow him, but proved unworthy of him and have passed away, and their names are writ in water. They had opportunities which they did not use. Work was allotted them which they were not worthy to take up. God said to them in answer to their request to be excused, "Ye shall be excused." They went back

> To the vile dust from whence they sprung,
> Unwept, unhonoured, and unsung.

But it shall not be so with you, my friends. Though I thus speak, I know your zeal and love and earnestness, and that you will continue to water others, and then you shall be watered yourselves. We will pray and strive together for the faith once delivered to the saints. We will cleave closer and closer to one another. Foot to foot, and shoulder to shoulder, we will march to battle for God and for His truth. Come what may, whoever may prove cravens in these days of charity and compromise, we will be found, in God's name, by the help of God's Spirit, faithful and true.

Water and Be Watered

And now, dear friends, another sentence or two will close the sermon. On the widest scale, this is true. This is true of our denomination, and of every Church. If we will water others, we shall be watered. From the very day when Carey, Fuller, and Pearce went forth to send the Gospel to the heathen, a blessing rested upon our denomination, I believe. If we had done more for the heathen, we should have been stronger to do more at home. You may rest assured, though some may not think it, that our missionary operations are an infinite blessing to the churches at home—that relinquishing them, giving them up, staying them, would bring such a blight and a curse that we had need to go down on our knees and pray, "God send the missionary work back again. Give us an outlet for our liberality and our zeal, for without it we become like a pool dammed up that is full of filth and toads and frogs and all sorts of foul things. Lord, open the river for our zeal and let us once again have an opportunity to serve You for the nations that are far away!" But I must leave *you* to preach on that point for my time has gone, and you can do so more practically than I can. My sermon is reported, and I will undertake that what you preach shall not be forgotten. It shall all be taken down in those boxes which shall be passed around. Say each of you as much as ever you can upon this subject by your contributions, and remember, "He that watereth others, shall himself be watered."

4

How a Man's Conduct Comes Home to Him

The backslider in heart shall be filled with his own ways: and a good man shall be satisfied from himself (Proverbs 14:14).

A common principle is here laid down and declared to be equally true in reference to two characters, who in other respects are a contrast. Men are affected by the course which they pursue, for good or bad their own conduct comes home to them. The backslider and the good man are very different, but in each of them the same rule is exemplified—they are both filled by the result of their lives. The backslider becomes filled by that which is within him as seen in his life, and the good man also is filled by that which grace implants within his soul. The evil leaven in the backslider leavens his entire being and sours his existence, while the gracious fountain in the sanctified believer saturates his whole manhood and baptizes his entire life. In each case the fullness arises from that which is within the man and is in its nature like the man's character. The fullness of the backslider's misery will come out of his own ways, and the fullness of the good man's content will spring out of the love of God which is shed abroad in his heart.

The meaning of this passage will come out better if we begin with an illustration. Here are two pieces of sponge, and we wish to fill them. You shall place one of them in a pool of foul water, and it will be filled with that which it lies in. You shall put the other sponge into a pure crystal stream, and it will also become full of the element in which it is placed. The backslider lies soaked in the dead sea of his own ways, and the brine fills him. The good man is plunged like a pitcher into "Siloa's brook, which flows hard by the oracle of God," and the river of the

---

This sermon was taken from *The Metropolitan Tabernacle Pulpit* and was preached on Sunday morning, May 16, 1875.

water of life fills him to the brim. A wandering heart will be filled with sorrow, and a heart confiding in the Lord will be satisfied with joy and peace. Or take two farmsteads: one farmer sows tares in his field, and in due time his barns are filled therewith. Another sows wheat, and his garners are stored with precious grain. Or follow out our Lord's parable: one builder places his frail dwelling on the sand. When the tempest rages, he is swept away in it. Naturally enough another lays deep the foundations of his house and sets it fast on a rock. As an equally natural consequence he smiles upon the storm, protected by his well-founded dwelling-place. What a man is by sin or by grace will be the cause of his sorrow or of his satisfaction.

The Backslider

I shall take the two characters without further preface. First let us speak awhile about the backslider. This is a very solemn subject, but one which it is needful to bring before the present audience, since we all have some share in it. I trust there may not be many present who are backsliders in the worst sense of the term, but very, very few among us are quite free from the charge of having backslidden, in some measure, at some time or other since conversion. Even those who sincerely love the Master sometimes wander, and we all need to take heed lest there be in any of us an evil heart of unbelief in departing from the living God.

There are several kinds of persons who may with more or less propriety be comprehended under the term "backsliders." These will each in his own measure be filled with his own ways.

There are, first, *apostates,* those who unite themselves with the church of Christ, and for a time act as if they were subjects of a real change of heart. These persons are frequently very zealous for a season and may become prominent, if not eminent, in the church of God. They did run well, like those mentioned by the apostle, but by some means they are, first of all, hindered, and slacken their pace. After that they linger and loiter, and leave the crown of the causeway for the side of the road. By-and-by in their hearts they go back into Egypt and at last, finding an opportunity to return, they break loose from all the restraints of their profession and openly forsake the Lord. Truly the last end of such men is worse than the first.

Judas is the great type of these preeminent backsliders. Judas was a professed believer in Jesus, a follower of the Lord, a minister of the Gospel, an apostle of Christ, the trusted treasurer of the college of the apostles, and after all turned out to be the "son of perdition" who sold his Master for thirty pieces of silver. He before long was filled with his own ways, for, tormented with remorse, he threw down the blood-money he had so dearly earned, hanged himself, and went to his own place. The story of Judas has been written over and over again in the lives of other traitors. We have heard of Judas as a deacon and as an elder. We have heard Judas preach. We have read the works of Judas the bishop and seen Judas the missionary. Judas sometimes continues in his profession for many years, but, sooner or later, the true character of the man is discovered. His sin returns upon his own head. If he does not make an end of himself, I do not doubt but what, even in this life, he often lives in such horrible remorse that his soul would choose strangling rather than life. He has gathered the grapes of Gomorra, and He has to drink the wine. He has planted a bitter tree, and he must eat the fruit thereof. Oh sirs, may none of you betray your Lord and Master. God grant I never may.

"Traitor! Traitor!" Shall that ever be written across your brow? You have been baptized into the name of the adorable Trinity. You have eaten the tokens of the Redeemer's body and blood. You have sung the songs of Zion. You have stood forward to pray in the midst of the people of God. Will you act so base a part as to betray your Lord? Shall it ever be said of you, "Take him to the place from whence he came, for he is a traitor?" I cannot conceive of anything more ignominious than for a soldier to be drummed out of a regiment of Her Majesty's soldiers, but what must it be to be cast out of the host of God! What must it be to be set up as the target of eternal shame and everlasting contempt for having crucified the Lord afresh and put Him to an open shame! How shameful will it be to be branded as an apostate from truth and holiness, from Christ and His ways. Better never to have made a profession than to have belied it so wretchedly, and to have it said of us, "it is happened unto them according to the true proverb, the dog is turned to his own vomit again; and the sow that was washed to her wallowing in the mire." Of such John has said, "They went out from us, but they were not of us for if they had been of us, they would no doubt have continued with us: but they went out, that they might be made manifest that they were not all of us."

This title of backslider applies also to another class, not so desperate but still most sad, of which not Judas but David may serve as the type. We refer to backsliders *who go into open sin*. There are men who descend from purity to careless living, from careless living to indulgence of the flesh, from indulgence of the flesh in little matters into known sin, and from one sin to another until they plunge into uncleanness. They have been born again; therefore the trembling and almost extinct life within must and shall revive and bring them to repentance. They will come back weary, weeping, humbled, and brokenhearted. They will be restored, but they will never be what they were before. Their voices will be hoarse, like that of David after his crime, for he never again sung so jubilantly as in his former days. Life will be more full of trembling and trial, and manifest less of buoyancy and joy of spirit. Broken bones make hard traveling, and even when they are set they are very subject to shooting pains when ill weathers are abroad.

I may be addressing some of this sort this morning, and if so I would speak with much faithful love. Dear brother, if you are now following Jesus afar off you will before long, like Peter, deny Him. Even though you will obtain mercy of the Lord, yet the text will certainly be fulfilled in you, and you will be "filled with your own ways." As certainly as Moses took the golden calf and ground it into powder, and then mixed it with the water which the sinful Israelites had to drink until they all tasted the grit in their mouths, so will the Lord do with you if you are indeed His child. He will take your idol of sin and grind it to powder, and your life shall be made bitter with it for years to come. When the gall and wormwood are most manifest in the cup of life it will be a mournful thing to feel "I procured this to myself by my shameful folly." O Lord, hold us up and keep us from falling by little and little, lest we plunge into overt sin and continue in it for a season. Surely the anguish which comes of such an evil is terrible as death itself. If David could rise from his grave and appear before you with his face seamed with sorrow and his brow wrinkled with his many griefs, he would say to you, "Keep your hearts with all diligence, lest ye bring woe upon your-selves. Watch as to prayer, and guard against the beginnings of sin lest your bones wax old through your roarings, and your moisture be turned into the drought of summer." O beware of a wandering heart, for it will be an awful thing to be filled with your own backslidings.

But there is a third sort of backsliding, and I am afraid a very large number of us have at times come under the title—I mean those *who in any measure of degree, even for a very little time, decline from the point which they have reached.* Perhaps such a man hardly ought to be called a backslider because it is not his predominant character, yet he back-slides. If he does not believe as firmly, love as intensely, and serve as zealously as he formerly did, he has in a measure backslidden. Any measure of backsliding, be it less or be it more, is sinful and will in pro-portion, as it is real backsliding, fill us with our own ways. If you only sow two or three seeds of the thistle there will not be so many of the ill weeds on your farm as if you had emptied out a whole sack, but still there will be enough and more than enough. Every little backsliding, as men call it, is a great mischief. Every little going back even *in heart* from God, if it never comes to words or deeds, yet will involve us in some measure of sorrow. If sin were clean removed from us, sorrow would be removed also. In fact, we should be in heaven, since a state of perfect holiness must involve perfect blessedness. Sin, in any degree, will bear its own fruit, and that fruit will be sure to set our teeth on edge. It is ill, therefore, to be a backslider even in the least degree.

Having said so much, let me now continue to think of the last two kinds of backsliders and leave out the apostate. Let us first *read his name,* and then let us read his history. We have both in our text.

The first part of his name is *"backslider."* He is not a back runner nor a back leaper, but a back*slider.* That is to say he slides back with an easy, effortless motion, softly, quietly, perhaps unsuspected by himself or anybody else. The Christian life is very much like climbing a hill of ice. You cannot slide up, no, you have to cut every step with an ice ax. Only with incessant labor in cutting and chipping can you make any progress. You need a guide to help you. You are not safe unless you are fastened to the guide, for you may slip into a crevasse. Nobody ever slides *up,* but if great care be not taken they will slide down, slide back, or in other words backslide. This is very easily done. If you want to know how to backslide, the answer is leave off going forward and you will slide backward—cease going upward and you will go downward of necessity, for stand still you never can.

To lead us to backslide, Satan acts with us as engineers do with a road down the mountain's side. If they desire to carry the road from yonder alp right down into the valley far below, they never think of making the road plunge over a precipice, or straight down the face of the rock, for nobody would ever use such a road. But the road makers wind and twist. See, the track descends very gently to the right, you can hardly see that it does run downward. Then it turns to the left with a small incline, and so, by turning this way and then that, the traveler finds himself in the vale below. Thus the crafty enemy of souls fetches saints down from their high places. Whenever he gets a good man down it is usually by slow degrees. Now and then, by sudden opportunity and strong temptation, the Christian man has been plunged right from the pinnacle of the temple into the dungeon of despair in a moment, but that is not often the case. The gentle decline is the Devil's favorite piece of engineering, and he manages it with amazing skill. The soul scarcely knows it is going down, it seems to be maintaining the even tenor of its way, but before long it is far below the line of peace and consecration.

Our dear brother, Dr. Arnot of the Free Church, illustrates this very beautifully by supposing a balance. This is the heavy scale loaded with seeds, and the other is high in the air. One morning you are very much surprised to find that what had been the heavier scale is aloft, while the other has descended. You do not understand it until you discover that certain little insects had silently transferred the seeds one by one. At first they made no apparent change. By-and-by there was a little motion, one more little seed was laid in the scales and the balance turned in a moment. Thus silently the balance of a man's soul may be affected and everything made ready for that one temptation by which the fatal turn is made, and the man becomes an open transgressor. Apparently insignificant agencies may gradually convey our strength from the right side to the wrong by grains and half-grains, until at last the balance is turned in the actual life and we are no more fit to be numbered with the visible saints of God.

Think again of this man's name. He is a "backslider," but what from? He is a man who knows the sweetness of the things of God and yet leaves off feeding upon them. He is one who has been favored to wait at the Lord's own table. Yet he deserts his honorable post, backslides from the things which he has known and felt and tasted and handled and rejoiced in—things that are the priceless gifts of God. He is a backslider from the condition in which he has enjoyed a heaven below. He is a backslider from the love of Him who bought him with His blood. He slides back from the wounds of Christ, from the words of the Eternal Spirit, from the crown of life that hangs over his head, and from a familiar relationship with God that angels might envy. Had he not been so highly favored he could not have been so basely wicked. O fool and slow of heart to slide from wealth to poverty; from health to disease; from liberty to bondage; from light to darkness; from the love of God, from abiding in Christ, and from the fellowship of the Holy Spirit to lukewarmness, worldliness, and sin.

The text, however, gives the man's name at greater length, *"The backslider in heart."* Now the heart is the fountain of evil. A man need not be a backslider in action to get the text fulfilled in him, he need only be a backslider in heart. All backsliding begins within, begins with the heart's growing lukewarm, begins with the love of Christ being less powerful in the soul. Perhaps you think that so long as backsliding is confined to the heart it does not matter much. But consider for a minute and you will confess your error. If you went to your physician and said, "Sir, I feel a severe pain in my body." Would you feel comforted if he replied, "There is no local cause for your suffering; it arises entirely from disease of the heart"? Would you not be far more alarmed than before? A case is serious indeed when it involves the heart. The heart is hard to reach and difficult to understand. Moreover it is so powerful over the rest of the system and has such power to injure all the members of the body, that a disease in the heart is an injury to a vital organ, a pollution of the springs of life. A wound—there are a thousand wounds—a complicated wounding of all the members at a stroke. Look well then to your hearts and pray, "O Lord, cleanse the secret parts of our spirit and preserve us to Your eternal kingdom and glory!"

Now let us *read this man's history*—"he shall be filled with his own ways." From which it is clear that he falls into ways of his own. When he was in his right state he followed the Lord's ways. He delighted himself in the law of the Lord, and He gave him the desire of his heart. But now he has ways of his own which he prefers to the ways of God. And what comes of this perverseness? Does he prosper? No; he is before long filled with his own ways. We will see what that means.

The first kind of fullness with his own ways is absorption in his carnal pursuits. He has not much time to spend upon religion. He has other things to attend to. If you speak to him of the deep things of God he is weary of you. Even of the daily necessaries of godliness he has no care to hear much, except at service time. He has his business to see to or he has to go out to a dinner party or a few friends are coming to spend the evening. In any case, his answer to you is, "I pray you have me excused." Now, this preoccupation with trifles is always mischievous, for when the soul is filled with chaff there is no room left for wheat. When all your mind is taken up with frivolities, the weighty matters of eternity cannot enter. Many professed Christians spend far too much time in amusements which they call recreation, but which, I fear, is far rather a redestruction than a recreation. The pleasures, cares, pursuits, and ambitions of the world swell in the heart when they once enter, and by-and-by they fill it completely. Like the young cuckoo in the sparrow's nest, worldliness grows and grows and tries its best to cast out the true owner of the heart. Whatever your soul is full of, if it be not full of Christ, it is in an evil case.

Then backsliders generally proceed a stage farther, and become full of their own ways by beginning to pride themselves upon their condition and to glory in their shame. Not that they really are satisfied at heart, on the contrary, they have a suspicion that things are not quite as they ought to be, and therefore they put on a bold front, and try to deceive themselves and others. It is rather dangerous to tell them of their faults, for they will not accept your rebuke, but will defend themselves, and even carry the war into your camp. They will say, "All of you are puritanical, strict and straight-laced, and your manners and ways do mischief rather than good." They would not bring up their children as you do yours, so they say. Their mouths are very full because their hearts are empty, and they talk very loudly in defense of themselves, because their conscience has been making a great stir within them. They call sinful pleasure a little unbending of the bow, greed is prudence, covetousness is economy, and dishonesty is cleverness. It is dreadful to think that men who know better should attempt thus to excuse themselves. Generally the warmest defender of a sinful practice is the man who has the most qualms of conscience about it. He himself knows that he is not living as he should, but he does not intend to cave in just yet, nor at all if he can help it. He is filled with his ways in a boasted self-content as to them.

Before long this fullness reaches another stage. If the backslider is a gracious man at all, he encounters chastisement, and that from a rod of his own making. A considerable time elapses before you can eat bread of your own growing: the ground must be plowed and sown. The wheat has to come up, to ripen and to be reaped, and threshed and ground in the mill. Then the flour must be kneaded and baked in the oven. Finally, the bread comes to the table and is eaten at last. Even so the backslider must eat of the fruit of his own ways. "Be not deceived; God is not mocked, whatsoever a man soweth, that shall he also reap."

Now look at the backslider eating the fruit of his ways. He neglected prayer, and when he tries to pray he cannot. His powers of desire, emotion, faith, and entreaty have failed. He kneels awhile, but he cannot pray. The Spirit of supplications is grieved and no longer helps his infirmities. He reaches down for his Bible and commences to read a chapter, but he has disregarded the Word of God so long that he finds it to be more like a dead letter than a living voice, though it used to be a sweet book before he became a backslider. The minister, too, is altered. He used to hear him with delight, but now the poor preacher has lost all his early power, so the backslider thinks. Other people do not think so, the place is just as crowded. There are as many saints edified and sinners saved as before. But the wanderer in heart began criticizing, and now he is entangled in the habit. He criticizes everything, but never feeds upon the truth at all. Like a madman at table he puts his fork into the morsel and holds it up, looks at it, finds fault with it, and throws it on the floor. Nor does he act better toward the saints in whose company he once delighted. They are dull society and he shuns them. Of all the things which bear upon his spiritual life he is weary, he has trifled with them and now he cannot enjoy them. Hear him sing, or rather sigh—

> Thy saints are comforted, I know,
> And love thy house of prayer;
> I sometimes go where others go,
> But find no comfort there.

How can it be otherwise? He is drinking water out of his own cistern and eating the bread of which he sowed the corn some years ago. His ways have come home to him.

Chastisement also comes out of his conduct in other ways. He was very worldly and gave great parties. Now his girls have grown up and grieved him by their conduct. He himself went into sin, and now that his sons outdo his example, what can he say? Can he wonder at anything? Look at David's case. David fell into a gross sin, and soon

Amnon his son rivaled him in iniquity. He murdered Uriah the Hittite, and Absalom murdered his brother Amnon. He rebelled against God, and lo, Absalom lifted up the standard of revolt against him. He disturbed the relationships of another man's family in a disgraceful manner. Now behold his own family rent in pieces and never restored to peace so that even when he lay a-dying he had to say, "My house is not so with God." He was filled with his own ways. It always will be so, even if the sin be forgotten. If you have sent forth a dove or a raven from the ark of your soul, it will come back to you just as you sent it out. May God save us from being backsliders lest the smooth current of our life should turn into a raging torrent of woe.

The fourth stage, blessed be God, is at length reached by gracious men and women, and what a mercy it is they ever do reach it! At last they become filled with their own ways in another sense—namely, satiated and dissatisfied, miserable and discontented. They sought the world and they gained it, but now it has lost all charms to them. They went after other lovers, but these deceivers have been false to them. They wring their hands and say, "Oh that I could return to my first husband for it was better with me then than now." Many have lived at a distance from Jesus Christ, but now they can bear it no longer. They cannot be happy until they return. Hear them cry in the language of the fifty-first psalm, "Restore unto me the joy of thy salvation; and uphold me with thy free spirit." But, I tell you, they cannot get back very easily. It is hard to retrace your steps from backsliding, even if it be but a small measure of it. But to get back from great wanderings is hard indeed, much harder than going over the road the first time. I believe that if the mental sufferings of some returning backsliders could be written and faithfully published they would astound you, and be a more horrible story to read than all the torments of the inquisition. What racks a man is stretched upon who has been unfaithful to his covenant with God! What fires have burned within the souls of those men who have been untrue to Christ and His cause! What dungeons, what grim and dark prisons under ground have saints of God lain in who have gone aside into By-path meadow instead of keeping to the king's highway. Their sighs and cries, for which after all they have learned to be thankful, are dolorous and terrible to listen to. They make us learn that he who sins must smart, and especially if he be a child of God. The Lord has said of His people, "You only have I known of all the people of the earth, therefore I will punish you for your iniquities." Whoever may go unchastised, a child of God never shall. The Lord will let His adversaries do a thousand things and not punish them in this life, since He reserves vengeance for them in the life to come. But as for His own children, they cannot sin without being visited with stripes.

Beloved friends, let all go straight away to the cross at once for fear we should be backsliders—

> Come, let us to the Lord our God
> With contrite hearts return;
> Our God is gracious, nor will leave
> The penitent to mourn.

Let us confess every degree and form of backsliding, every wandering of heart, every decline of love, every wavering of faith, every flagging of zeal, every dullness of desire, every failure of confidence. Behold, the Lord says to us, "Return"; therefore let us return. Even if we be not backsliders it will do us no hurt to come to the cross as penitents, indeed, it is well to abide there evermore. O Spirit of the living God, preserve us in believing penitence all our days.

The Christian

I have but little time for the second part of my subject. Excuse me therefore if I do not attempt to go into it very deeply. As it is true of the backslider that he grows at last full of that which is within him and his wickedness, is true also of the Christian that in pursuing the paths of righteousness and the way of faith, he becomes filled and contented too. That which grace has placed within him fills him in due time.

Here then we have the good man's name and history.

Notice first, his name. It is a very remarkable thing that a backslider if you call out his name will not as a rule answer to it, even so a good man will not acknowledge the title here assigned him. Where is the good man? I know that every man here who is right before God will pass the question on saying, "There is none good save One, that is God." The good man will also question my text and say, "I cannot feel satisfied with myself." No, dear friend, but mind you read the words aright. It does not say "satisfied *with* himself," no truly good man ever was self-satisfied, and when they talk as if they are self-satisfied it is time to doubt whether they know much about the matter. All the good men I have ever met with have always wanted to be better. They have longed for something higher than as yet they have reached. They would not own to it that they were satisfied, and they certainly were by no means satisfied with themselves. The text does not say that they are, but it says something that reads so much like it that care is needed.

Now, if I should seem to say this morning that a good man looks within and is quite satisfied with what he finds there, please let me say at once, I mean nothing of the sort. I should like to say exactly what the text means, but I do not know quite whether I shall manage to do it, except you will help me by not misunderstanding me, even if there should be a strong temptation to do so. Here is the good man's history, he is "satisfied *from* himself." But first I must read his name again, though he does not own to it, what is he good for? He says, "good for nothing," but in truth he is good for much when the Lord uses him. Remember that he is good because the Lord has made him over again by the Holy Spirit. Is not that good which God makes? When he created nature at the first he said of all things that they were very good. How could they be otherwise, since He made them? So in the new creation a new heart and right spirit are from God, and must be good. Where there is grace in the heart the grace is good and makes the heart good. A man who has the righteousness of Jesus and the indwelling of the Holy Spirit is good in the sight of God.

A good man is on the side of good. If I were to ask, who is on the side of good? we would not pass on that question. No, we would step out and say, "I am. I am not all I ought to be or wish to be, but I am on the side of justice, truth, and holiness. I would live to promote goodness and even die rather than become the advocate of evil." And what is the man who loves that which is good? Is he evil? I know not. He who truly loves that which is good must be in a measure good himself. Who is he that strives to be good, and groans and sighs over his failures, yes and rules his daily life by the laws of God? Is he not one of the world's best men? I trust without self-righteousness the grace of God has made some of us good in this sense, for what the Spirit of God has made is good, and if in Christ Jesus we are new creatures, we cannot contradict Solomon, nor criticize the Bible if it calls such persons good, though we dare not call ourselves good.

Now, a good man's history is this, "He is satisfied from himself."

That means first, that he is independent of outward circumstances. He does not derive satisfaction from his birth or honors or properties, but that which fills him with content is within himself. Our hymn puts it so truly—

> I need not go abroad for joys,
>   I have a feast at home,
> My sighs are turned into songs,
>   My heart has ceased to roam.
>
> Down from above the blessed Dove
>   Is come into my breast,
> To witness thine eternal love
>   And give my spirit rest.

Other men must bring music from abroad if they have any, but in the gracious man's bosom there lives a little bird that sings sweetly to him.

He has a flower in his own garden more sweet than any he could buy in the market or find in the king's palace. He may be poor, but still he would not change his estate in the kingdom of heaven for all the grandeur of the rich. His joy and peace are not even dependent upon the health of his body. He is often well in soul when sick as to his flesh; he is frequently full of pain and yet perfectly satisfied. He may carry about with him an incurable disease which he knows will shorten and eventually end his life, but he does not look to this poor life for satisfaction, he carries that within him which creates immortal joy. The love of God shed abroad in his soul by the Holy Spirit yields a perfume sweeter than the flowers of Paradise. The fulfillment of the text is partly found in the fact that the good man is independent of his surroundings.

And he is also independent of the praise of others. The backslider keeps easy because the minister thinks well of him and Christian friends think well of him, but the genuine Christian who is living near to God thinks little of the verdict of men. What other people think of him is not his chief concern. He is sure that he is a child of God. He knows he can say, "Abba, Father." He glories that for him to live is Christ, and to die is gain. Therefore he does not need the approbation of others to buoy up his confidence. He runs alone, and does not need, like a weakly child, to be carried in arms. He knows whom he has believed, and his heart rests in Jesus. Thus he is satisfied, not from other people and from their judgment, but "from himself."

Then, again, the Christian man is content with the well of upspringing water of life which the Lord has placed within him. There, my friends, up on the everlasting hills is the divine reservoir of all-sufficient grace, and down here in our bosom is a spring which bubbles up to everlasting life. It has been welling up in some of us these twenty-five years, but why is it so? The grand secret is that there is an unbroken connection between the little spring within the renewed breast and that vast unfathomed fount of God. Because of this the well-spring never fails in summer and in winter it still continues to flow. And now if you ask me if I am dissatisfied with the spring within my soul which is fed by the all-sufficiency of God, I reply, no, I am not. If you could by any possibility cut the connection between my soul and my Lord I should despair altogether. But as long as none can separate me from the love of God, which is in Christ Jesus our Lord, I am satisfied and at rest. Like Naphtali we are "satisfied with favour and full of the blessing of the Lord."

Faith is in the good man's heart and he is satisfied with what faith brings him, for it conveys to him the perfect pardon of his sin. Faith brings him nearer to Christ. Faith brings him adoption into the family of God. Faith secures him conquest over temptation. Faith procures for him everything he requires. He finds that by believing he has all the blessings of the covenant daily to enjoy. Well may he be satisfied with such an enriching grace. The just shall live by faith.

In addition to faith, he has another filling grace called hope which reveals to him the world to come, and gives him assurance that when he falls asleep he will sleep in Jesus, and that when he awakes he will arise in the likeness of Jesus. Hope delights him with the promise that his body shall rise, and that in his flesh he shall see God. This hope of his sets the pearly gates wide open before him, reveals the streets of gold, and makes him hear the music of the celestial harpers. Surely a man may well be satisfied with this.

The godly heart is also satisfied with what love brings him. For love, though it seem but a gentle maid, is strong as a giant and becomes in some respects the most potent of all the graces. Love first opens wide herself like the flowers in the sunshine and drinks in the love of God, and then she joys in God and begins to sing—

I am so glad that Jesus loves me.

She loves Jesus. There is such an interchange of delight between the love of her soul to Christ and the love of Christ to her, that heaven itself can scarce be sweeter. He who knew this deep mysterious love will be more than filled with it, he will need to be enlarged to hold the bliss which it creates. The love of Jesus is known, but yet it passes knowledge. It fills the entire man so that he has no room for the idolatrous love of the creature. He is satisfied from himself and asks no other joy.

Beloved, when the good man is enabled by divine grace to live in obedience to God, he must, as a necessary consequence, enjoy peace of mind. His hope is alone fixed on Jesus, but a life which evidences his possession of salvation casts many a sweet ingredient into his cup. He who takes the yoke of Christ upon him and learns of Him finds rest to his soul. When we keep His commandments we consciously enjoy His love, which we could not do if we walked in opposition to His will. To know that you have acted from a pure motive, to know that you have done the right, is a grand means of full content. What matters the frown of foes or the prejudice of friends, if the testimony of a good conscience is heard within? We dare not rely upon our own works, neither have we had any desire or need to do so, for our Lord Jesus has saved us everlastingly. Still, "Our rejoicing is this, the testimony of our conscience, that in simplicity and godly sincerity, not with fleshly wisdom, but by the grace of God, we have had our conversation in the world."

The Christian needs to maintain unbroken fellowship with Jesus, his Lord, if he would be good as a soldier of Christ. But if his communion be broken his satisfaction will depart. If Jesus be within we shall be satisfied from within, but not else. If our fellowship with Him be kept up, and it may be found day to day, and month to month, and year to year (and why should it ever be snapped at all), then the satisfaction will continue, and the soul will continue to be full even to the brim with the bliss which God alone can give. If we are by the Holy Spirit made to be abundant in labor or patient in suffering, if, in a word, we resign ourselves fully up to God, we shall find a fullness of his grace placed within ourselves. An enemy compared some of us to cracked vessels, and we may humbly accept the description. We do find it difficult to retain good things. They run away from our leaking pitchers. But I will tell how a cracked pitcher can be kept continually full. Put it in the bottom of an ever-flowing river, and it must be full. Even so though we are leaking and broken, if we abide in the love of Christ we shall be filled with His fullness. Such an experience is possible. We may be

> Plunged in the Godhead's deepest sea,
> And lost in his immensity.

Then we shall be full, full to running over. As the psalmist says, "my cup runneth over." The man who walks in God's ways obediently resting wholly upon Christ, looking for all His supplies to the great eternal deeps, that is the man who will be filled, filled with the very things which he has chosen for his own, filled with those things which are his daily delight and desire. Well may the faithful believer be filled, for he has eternity to fill him. The Lord has loved him with an everlasting love. There is the eternity past: "The mountains shall depart and the hills be removed, but my covenant shall not depart from thee"—there is the eternity to come. He has infinity, yes the infinite One himself, for the Father is his Father, the Son is his Savior, the Spirit of God dwells within him—the Trinity may well fill the heart of man. The believer has omnipotence to fill him, for all power is given to Christ, and of that power Christ will give to us according as we have need. Living in Christ and hanging upon Him from day to day, beloved, we shall have a "peace of God which passeth all understanding to keep our hearts and minds through Christ Jesus." May we enjoy this peace and magnify the name of the Lord forever and ever. Amen.

5

God, the All-Seeing One

Hell and destruction are before the LORD: *how much more then the hearts of the children of men?* (*Proverbs 15:11*).

You have often smiled at the ignorance of heathens who bow themselves before gods of wood and stone. You have quoted the words of Scripture and have said, "Eyes have they, but they see not; ears have they, but they hear not." You have therefore argued that they could not be gods at all because they could neither see nor hear, and you have smiled contemptuously at the men who could so debase their understandings as to make such things objects of adoration. May I ask you one question—but one? Your God can both see and hear: would your conduct be in any respect different if you had a god such as those that the heathen worship? Suppose for one minute that Jehovah, who is nominally adored in this land, could be (though it is almost blasphemy to suppose it) smitten with such a blindness that He could not see the works and know the thought of man. Would you then become more careless concerning Him than you are now? I know not. In nine cases out of ten, and perhaps in a far larger and sadder proportion, the doctrine of Divine Omniscience, although it is received and believed, has no practical effect upon our lives at all. The mass of mankind forget God. Whole nations who know His existence and believe that He beholds them live as if they had no God at all. Merchants, farmers, men in their shops and in their fields, husbands in their families, and wives in the midst of their households live as if there were no God—no eye inspecting them, no ear listening to the voice of their lips, and no eternal mind always treasuring up the recollection of their acts. Ah! we are practical atheists, the mass of us. Yes, all but those that have been born again and have passed from death to life, be their creeds what they may,

This sermon was taken from *The New Park Street Pulpit* and was preached on Sunday morning, February 14, 1858.

are atheists, after all, in life. For if there were no God and no hereafter, multitudes of men would never be affected by the change. They would live the same as they do now—their lives being so full of disregard of God and His ways, that the absence of God could not affect them in any great degree. Permit me, then, this morning, as God shall help me, to stir up your hearts. May God grant that something I may say, may drive some of your practical atheism out of you. I would endeavor to set before you, God the all-seeing one, and press upon your solemn consideration the tremendous fact that in all our acts, in all our ways, and in all our thoughts, we are continually under His observing eye.

We have in our text, first of all, *a great fact declared*—"Hell and destruction are before the Lord." We have, secondly, *a great fact inferred*—"How much more then the hearts of the children of men?"

A Great Fact Declared

We will begin with the great fact which is declared—a fact which furnishes us with premises from which we deduce the practical conclusion of the second sentence—"How much more then the hearts of the children of men?" The best interpretation that you can give of those two words, "hell" and "destruction," is, I think, comprehended in a sentence something like this—*Death and hell are before the Lord.* The separate state of departed spirits and destruction, *Abaddon,* as the Hebrew has it, the place of torment, are both of them, although solemnly mysterious to us, manifest enough to God.

First, then, the word here translated *hell* might just as well be translated "death," or the state of departed spirits. Now, death, with all its solemn consequences, is visible before the Lord. Between us and the hereafter of departed spirits a great black cloud is hanging. Here and there, the Holy Spirit has made chinks, as it were, in the black wall of separation, through which by faith we can see. For He has "revealed unto us by the Spirit" the things which "eye hath not seen nor ear heard," and which the human intellect could never compass. Yet, what we know is but very little. When men die, they pass beyond the realm of our knowledge: both in body and in soul they go beyond our understandings. But God understands all the secrets of death. Let us divide these into several heads and enumerate them.

God knows the burial places of all His people. He notes as well the resting place of the man who is buried tombless and alone, as the man over whom a mighty mausoleum has been raised. The traveler who fell in the barren desert, whose body became the prey of the vulture and whose bones were bleached in the sun—the mariner who was wrecked far out at sea and over whose corpse no dirge was ever wailed, except the howling of the winds and the murmuring of the wild waves—the thousands who have perished in battle, unnumbered and unnoticed—the many who have died alone amid dreary forests, frozen seas, and devouring snowstorms—all those, and the places of their sepulcher, are known to God. That silent grotto within the sea, where pearls lie deep, where now the shipwrecked one is sleeping, is marked by God as the death-place of one of His redeemed. That place upon the mountainside, the deep ravine into which the traveler fell and was buried in a snow-drift, is marked in the memory of God as the tomb of one of the human race. No body of man, however it may have been interred or uninterred, has passed beyond the range of God's knowledge.

Blessed be His name if I shall die and lie where the rude forefathers of the hamlet sleep in some neglected corner of the churchyard, I shall be known as well and rise as well recognized by my glorious Father as if interred in the cathedral where forests of gothic pillars proudly stand erect, and where the songs of myriads perpetually salute high heaven. I shall be known as well as if I had been buried there in solemn pomp, and had been interred with music and with dread solemnities, and I shall be recognized as well as if the marble trophy and the famous pillar had been raised to my remembrance. For God knows no such thing as forgetfulness of the burying places of His children. Moses sleeps in some spot that eye has not seen. God kissed away his soul, He buried him where Israel could never find him, though they may have searched for him. But God knows where Moses sleeps. If He knows that, He understands where all His children are hidden. You cannot tell me where is the tomb of Adam. You could not point out to me the sleeping place of Abel. Is any man able to discover the tomb of Methuselah and those long-lived dwellers in the time before the flood? Who shall tell where the once-treasured body of Joseph now sleeps in faith? Can any of you discover the tombs of the kings, and mark the exact spot where David and Solomon rest in solitary grandeur? No, those things have passed from human recollection. We know not where the great and mighty of the past are buried, but God knows for death and Hades are open before the Lord.

And again, further, not only does he know the place where they were buried, but he is cognizant of the history of all their bodies after sepulture or after death. It has often been asked by the infidel, "How can the body of man be restored when it may have been eaten by the cannibal or devoured by wild beasts?" Our simple reply is that God can track every atom of it if He pleases. We do not think it necessary to resurrection that He should do so, but if He so willed it, he could bring every atom of every body that has ever died. Although it has passed through the most complicated machinery of nature, and become entangled in its passage with plants and beasts, yes, and with the bodies of other men, God has it still within the range of His knowledge to know where every atom is. It is within the might of his Omnipotence to call every atom from its wandering, and restore it to its proper sphere, and rebuild the body of which it was a part. It is true, we could not track the dust that long since has moldered. Buried with exactest care, preserved with the most scrupulous reverence, years passed away and the body of the monarch, which had long slept well-guarded and protected, was at last reached by the careless hand. The coffin had moldered, and the metal was broken for the sake of its own value. A handful of dust was discovered, the last relics of one who was master of many nations. That dust by sacrilegious hand was cast in the aisle of the church, or thrown into the churchyard and blown by the winds into the neighboring field. It was impossible forever to preserve it; the greatest care was defeated. At last the monarch was on a level with his slave, "alike unknowing and unknown." But God knows where every particle of the handful of dust has gone. He has marked in His book the wandering of every one of its atoms. He has death so open before His view that He can bring all these together, bone to bone, and clothe them with the very flesh that robed them in the days of yore, and make them live again. Death is open before the Lord.

And as the body, so the soul when separated from the body is before the Lord. We look upon the countenance of our dying friend, and on a sudden a mysterious change passes over his frame. "His soul has fled," we say. But have we any idea of what his soul is? Can we form even a conjecture of what the flying of that soul may be, and what the august presence into which it is ushered when it is disentangled from its earthly coil? Is it possible for us to guess what is that state where spirits without bodies, perpetually blessed, behold their God? It is possible for us to compass some imagination of what heaven is to be, when bodies and souls, reunited, shall before God's throne enjoy the highest bliss. But I do think, that so gross are our conceptions, while we are in our bodies that it is almost, if not quite, impossible for any of us to form any idea whatever as to the position of souls while in the disembodied state, between the hour of death and the time of resurrection.

> This much, and this is all, we know,
>   They are supremely blest;
> Have done with sin, and care, and woe,
>   And with their Saviour rest.

But the best of the saints can tell us nothing more than this. They are blessed and in paradise they are reigning with their Lord. Friends, these things are known to God. The separate state of the dead, the heaven of disembodied spirits, is within the gaze of the Most High. At this hour, if so He pleased, He could reveal to us the condition of every man that is dead—whether he has mounted to Elysian fields to dwell forever in the sunlight of his Master's countenance, or has been plunged into hell, dragged down by iron chains to wait in dreary woe the result of the awful trial when "Depart ye cursed" must be the reaffirmation of a sentence once pronounced and already in part endured. God understands the separate doom of every man's spirit before the great tribunal day—before the last sentence shall have been pronounced, death is open before the Lord.

The next word, *destruction,* signifies hell, or the place of the damned. That also is open before the Lord. Where hell is and what its miseries, we know not, except "through a glass darkly," we have never seen the invisible things of horror. That land of terror is a land unknown. We have much reason to thank God that He has put it so far off from the habitations of living mortals that the pains, the groans, the shrieks, the yells are not to be heard here, or else earth itself would have become a hell, the solemn prelude and the ante-past of unutterable torment. God has put somewhere, far on the edge of His dominions, a fearful lake that burns with fire and brimstone. Into that He cast the rebel angels, who (though by a license they are now allowed to walk the earth) do carry a hell within their bosoms, and are by-and-by to be bound with chains, reserved in blackness and darkness forever for them that kept not their first estate, but lifted the arm of their rebellion against God. Into that place we dare not look. Perhaps it would not be possible for any man to get a fair idea of the torments of the lost, without at once becoming mad. Reason would reel at such a sight of horror. One moment of listening to the shrill screams of spirits tortured might forever drive us into the depths of despair and make us only fit to be bound in chains while we lived on earth. Raving lunatics surely we must become. But while God has mercifully covered all these things from us, they are all known to Him. He looks upon them; yes, it is His look that makes hell what it is. His eyes, full of fury, flash the lightnings that scathe His enemies; His lips, full of dreadful thunders, make the thunders that now affright the wicked. Oh! could they escape the eye of God, could they shut out that dreary vision of the face of the incensed Majesty of heaven, then might hell be quenched; then might the wheels of Ixion stand still; then might doomed Tantalus quench his thirst and eat to his very full. But there, while they lie in their chains, they look upward and see ever that fearful vision of the Most High; the dreadful hails that grasp the thunderbolts, the dreadful lips that speak the thunders, and the fearful eyes that flash the flames that burn their souls, with horrors deeper than despair. Yes, hell, horrible as it is and veiled in many clouds and covered over with darkness, is naked before the vision of the Most High.

There is the grand fact stated—"Hell and destruction are before the Lord." After this the inference seems to be easy—"How much more then the hearts of the children of men?"

The Great Fact Inferred

In briefly entering upon this second part I will discuss the subject thus: You notice there an argument—"How much more then the hearts of the children of men?" I will therefore begin by asking, why does it follow that the hearts of men are seen by God? *Why—how—what—when*—shall be four questions into which we shall divide what we have now to say.

Why is it so clear, that "if hell and destruction are open before the Lord," the hearts of men must be very plainly viewed by Him?

We answer, because the hearts of men are not so extensive as the realms of death and torment. What is man's heart? What is man's self? Is he not in Scripture compared to a grasshopper? Does not God declare that he "takes up the isles"—whole islands full of men—"as a very little thing. And the nations before him are but as the drop of a bucket"? If then, the all-seeing eye of God takes in at one glance the wide region's of death—and wide they are, wide enough to startle any man who shall try to range them through—if I say, with one glance God sees death and sees hell through with all its bottomless depths, with all its boundlessness of misery, surely, then, He is quite able to behold all the actions of the little thing called man's heart. Suppose a man so wise as to be able to know the wants of a nation and to remember the feelings of myriads of men, you cannot suppose it difficult for him to know the actions of his own family and to understand the emotions of his own household. If the man is able to stretch his arm over a great sphere and to say, "I am monarch of all this," surely he shall be able to control the less. He who in his wisdom can walk through centuries shall not say that he is ignorant of the history of a year. He who can dive into the depths of science and understand the history of the whole world from its creation is not to be alarmed by some small riddle that happens at his own door. No, the God who sees death and hell sees our hearts, for they are far less extensive.

Reflect again that they are far less aged too. Death is an ancient monarch, he is the only king whose dynasty stands fast. Ever since the days of Adam he has never been succeeded by another, and has never had an interregnum in his reign. His black ebony scepter has swept away generation after generation. His scythe has mowed the fair fields of this earth a hundred times and is sharp to mow us down. When another crop shall succeed us he is still ready to devour the multitudes and sweep the earth clean again. The regions of death are old domains. His pillars of black granite are ancient as the eternal hills. Death made his prey on earth long before Adam was here. Those mighty creatures that made the deep hoary with their strength, and stirred the earth with their tramplings—those elder born of nature's sons, the mighty creatures that lived here long before Adam walked in Eden—death made them his prey. Like a mighty hunter he speared the mighty lizard and laid it low, and now we dig it from the stony tomb and wonder at it. He is our ancient monarch. But ancient as he is, his whole monarchy is in the records of God, and until death itself is dead and swallowed up in victory, death shall be open before the Lord. How old, too, is hell!—old as the first sin. In that day when Satan tempted the angels and led astray the third part of the stars of heaven, then hell was digged. Then was that bottomless pit first struck out of solid rocks of vengeance that it might stand a marvelous record of what God's wrath can do. The fires of hell are not the kindlings of yesterday, they are ancient flames that burned long before Vesuvius cast forth its lurid flame. Long before the first charred ashes fell upon the plain from earth's red volcanoes, hell's flames were burning. For "Tophet is prepared of old, the pile thereof is fire and much wood; the breath of the Lord like a stream of brimstone, doth kindle it."

If, then, the ancient things, these old ones, death and hell, have been observed by God, and if their total history is known to Him, how much more then shall He know the history of that mere animalcule, that ephemera of an hour, that we call man? You are here today and gone tomorrow, born yesterday—the next hour shall see our tomb prepared, and another minute shall hear, "ashes to ashes, dust to dust," and the falling of the clod upon the coffin lid. We are the creatures of a day and know nothing. We are scarcely here; we are only living and dead. "Gone!" is the greatest part of our history. Scarcely have we time enough to tell the story before it comes to its finish. Surely, then, God may easily understand the history of a man when He knows the history of the monarchies of death and hell.

This is the *why*. I need not give further arguments, though there be abundance deducible from the text. "How much more then the hearts of the children of men?"

But now, *how* does God know the heart? I mean to what degree and to what extent does He understand and know that which is in man? I answer, Holy Scripture in divers places gives us most precise information. God knows the heart so well that He is said to "search" it. We all understand the figure of a search. There is a search-warrant out against some man who is supposed to be harboring a traitor in his house. The officer goes into the lower room, opens the door of every cupboard, looks into every closet, and peers into every cranny. Then he takes the key, descends into the cellar, turns over the coals, disturbs the wood, lest anyone should be hidden there. Upstairs he goes; there is an old room that has not been opened for years—it is opened. There is a huge chest; the lock is forced and it is broken open. The very top of the house is searched, lest upon the slates or upon the tiles someone should be concealed. At last, when the search has been complete, the officer says, "It is impossible that there can be anybody here, for, from the tiles to the foundation, I have searched the house thoroughly through. I know the very spiders well, for I have seen the house completely." Now, it is just so that God knows our heart. He searches it—searches into every nook, corner, crevice and secret part; and the figure of the Lord is pushed further still. "The candle of the Lord," we are told, "searches the secret parts of the belly." As when we wish to find something, we take a candle and look down upon the ground with great care and turn up the dust. If it is some little piece of money we desire to find, we light a candle and sweep the house and search diligently until we find it. Even so it is with God. He searches Jerusalem with candles, and pulls everything to daylight. No partial search, like that of Laban when he went into Rachel's tent to look for his idols. She put them in the camel's furniture and sat upon them; but God looks into the camel's furniture and all. "Can any hide himself in secret places, that I shall not see him? says the Lord." His eye searches the heart and looks into every part of it.

In another passage we are told that God tries the reins. That is even more than searching. The goldsmith when he takes gold looks at it and examines it carefully. "Ah!" says he, "but I don't understand this gold yet. I must try it." He thrusts it into the furnace; there coals are heaped upon it, and it is fused and melted until he knows what there is of dross, and what there is of gold. Now, God knows to the very carat how much there is of sound gold in us and how much of dross. There is no deceiving Him. He has put our hearts into the furnace of His Omniscience: the furnace—His knowledge—tries us as completely as the goldsmith's crucible does try the gold—how much there is of hypocrisy, how much of truth, how much of sham, how much of real—how much of ignorance, how much of knowledge—how much of devotion, how much of blasphemy—how much of carefulness, how much of carelessness. God knows the ingredients of the heart. He reduces the soul to its pristine metals. He divides it asunder—so much of quartz, so much of gold, so much of dung, of dross, of wood, of hay, of stubble, so much of gold, silver, and precious stones. "The Lord trieth the hearts and searcheth the reins of the children of men."

Here is another description of God's knowledge of the heart. In one place of Sacred Writ (it will be well if you set your children to fill out these places at home) God is said to ponder the heart. Now, you know, the Latin word *ponder* means *weigh*. The Lord weighs the heart. Old Master Quarles has gotten a picture of a great one putting a heart into one scale, and then putting the law, the Bible, into the other scale, to weigh it. This is what God does with men's hearts. They are often great, puffed-up, blown out things, and people say, "What a great-hearted man that is!" But God does not judge by the appearance of a man's great heart nor the outside appearance of a good heart. But He puts it in the scales and weighs it—puts His own Word in one scale and the heart in the other. He knows the exact weight—knows whether we have grace in the heart, which makes us good weight, or only pretense in the heart, which makes us weigh light weight when put into the scale. He searches the heart in every possible way. He puts it into the fire and then thrusts it into the balances. Oh, might not God say of many of you, "I have searched your heart, and I have found vanity therein? Reprobate silver shall men call you; for God has put you in the furnace and rejected you." And then He might conclude His verdict by saying, "*Mene, mene tekel*—thou art weighed in the balances and found wanting." This, then, is the answer to the question, *how?*

The next question is, *what?* What is it that God sees in man's heart? God sees in man's heart a great deal more than we think. God sees, and has seen in our hearts, lust, blasphemy, murder, adultery, malice, wrath, and all uncharitableness. The heart never can be painted too black unless you daub it with something blacker than the Devil himself. It is as base as it can be. You have never committed murder, but yet you have had murder in your heart. You may never have stained your hands with lust and the aspersions of uncleanness, but still it is in the heart. Have you never imagined an evil thing? Has your soul never for a moment doted on a pleasure which you were too chaste to indulge in, but which for a moment you surveyed with at least some little complacency and delight? Has not imagination often pictured, even to the solitary monk in his cell, greater vice than men in public life have ever dreamed of? And may not even the divine in his closet be conscious that blasphemies and murders and lusts of the vilest class can find a ready harbor even in the heart which he hopes is dedicated to God? Oh! beloved, it is a sight that no human eye could endure. The sight of a heart really laid bare before one's own inspection would startle us almost into insanity. But God sees the heart in all its bestial sensuousness, in all its wanderings and rebellions, in all its highmindedness and pride. God has searched and knows it altogether.

God sees all the heart's imaginations, and what they are let us not presume to tell. O children of God, these have made you cry and groan full many a time, and though the worldling groans not over them, yet he has them. Oh, what a filthy sty of Stygian imaginations is the heart. All full of everything that is hideous when it once begins to dance and make carnival and revelry concerning sin. But God sees the heart's imaginations.

Again, God sees the heart's devices. You perhaps, O sinner, have determined to curse God. You have not done so, but you intend to do it. He knows your devices—reads them all. You perhaps will not be permitted to run into the excess of riotousness into which you purpose to go, but your very purpose is now undergoing the inspection of the Most High. There is never a design forged in the fires of the heart before it is beaten on the anvil of resolve, that is not known, and seen, and rioted by Jehovah our God.

He knows, next, the resolves of the heart. He knows, O sinner, how many times you have resolved to repent, and have resolved and re-resolved, and then have continued the same. He knows, O you that have been sick, how you did resolve to seek God, but how you did despise your own resolution when good health had put you beyond the temporary danger. Your resolves have been filed in heaven. Your broken promises and vows despised shall be brought out in their order as swift witnesses for your condemnation. All these things are known of God. We have often had very clear proof of God's knowing what is in man's heart, even in the ministry. Some months ago, while standing here preaching, I deliberately pointed to a man in the midst of the crowd and said these words, "There is a man sitting there that is a shoemaker who keeps his shop open on Sunday. He had his shop open last Sabbath morning, took nine pence, and there was four pence profit out of it. His soul is sold to Satan for four pence." A City Missionary when going around the west end of the town, met with a poor man of whom he asked this question, "Do you know Mr. Spurgeon?" He found him reading a sermon. "Yes," he said, "I have every reason to know him. I have been to hear him, and under God's grace I have become a new man. But," said he, "shall I tell you how it was? I went to the Music Hall and took my seat in the middle of the place, and the man looked at me as if he knew me. He deliberately told the congregation that I was a shoemaker and that I sold shoes on a Sunday. I did, sir. But, sir, I should not have minded that; but he said I took nine pence the Sunday before and that there was four pence profit. I did take nine pence, and four pence was just the profit. How he should know that I'm sure I cannot tell. It struck me it was God had spoken to my soul through him. I shut up my shop last Sunday, and was afraid to open it and go there lest he should split about me again." I could tell as many as a dozen authentic stories of cases that have happened in this hall where I have deliberately pointed at somebody, without the slightest knowledge of the person or ever having in the least degree any inkling or idea that what I said was right, except that I believed I was moved thereto by the Spirit. So striking has been the description that the persons have gone away and said, "Come, see a man that told me all things that ever I did. He was sent of God to my soul, beyond a doubt, or else he could not have painted my case so clearly."

And not only so, but we have known cases in which the thoughts of men have been revealed from the pulpit. I have sometimes seen persons nudge with their elbow because they have gotten a smart hit, and I have heard them say when they went out, "That is just what I said to you when I went in at the door." "Ah!" says the other, "I was thinking of the very thing he said, and he told me of it." Now, if God thus proves His own Omniscience by helping His poor, ignorant servant to state the very thing, thought and done, when he did not know it, then it must remain decisively proved that God does know everything that is secret because we see He tells it to men and enables them to tell it to others. Oh, you may endeavor as much as you can to hide your faults from God, but beyond a doubt He shall discover you. He discovers you this day. His Word is "a discerner of the thoughts and intents of the heart," and "pierces to the dividing asunder of the joints and of the marrow." In that last day when the book shall be opened, and He shall give to every man his sentence, then shall it be seen how exact, how careful, how precious, how personal was God's knowledge of the heart of every man whom He had made.

And, now, the last question: *when?* When does God see us? The answer is, he sees us everywhere and in every place. O foolish man, who thinks to hide himself from the Most High! It is night; no human eye sees you. The curtain is drawn, and you are hidden. There are His eyes lowering at you through the gloom. It is a far-off country; no one knows you. Parents and friends have been left behind, restraints are cast off. There is a Father near you who looks upon you even now. It is a lone spot, and if the deed be done, no tongue shall tell it. There is a tongue in heaven that shall tell it. Yes, the beam out of the wall and the stones in the field shall raise up themselves as witnesses against you. Can you hide yourself anywhere where God shall not detect you? Is not this whole world like a glass hive wherein we put our bees? And does not God stand and see all our motions when we think we are hidden? Ah, it is but a glass hiding place. He looks from heaven, and through stone walls and rocks; yes, to the very center itself does His eye pierce, and in the thickest darkness He beholds our deeds.

Come, then, let me make a personal application of the matter, and I have done. If this be true, hypocrite, what a fool you are! If God can read the heart, O man, what a sorry, sorry thing your fair pretense must be! Ah! ah! ah! what a change will come over some of you! This world is a masquerade, and you, many of you, wear the mask of religion. You dance your giddy hours and men think you to be the saints of God. How changed will you be, when, at the door of eternity, you must drop the visor and must renounce the theatricals in which you live! How you will blush when the paint is washed from off your cheek—when you stand before God naked to your own shame, a hypocrite, unclean, diseased, covered up before with the gew-gaws and the trickery of pretended formality in religion, but now standing there, base, vile, and hideous! There is many a man that tears about him a cancer that would make one sick to see. Oh! how shall hypocrites look when their cancerous hearts are laid bare! Deacon! how you will tremble when your old heart is torn open, and your vile pretenses rent away! Minister! how black you will look when your surplice is off and when your grand pretensions are cast to the dogs! How will you tremble! There will be no sermonizing others then. You yourself will be preached to and the sermon shall be from that text, "Depart, ye cursed." O friends, above all things shun hypocrisy. If you mean to be damned, make up your minds to it and be damned like honest men. But do not, I beseech you, pretend to go to heaven, while all the while you are going to hell. If you mean to make your abodes in torment forever, then serve the Devil and do not be ashamed of it. Stand it right out and let the world know what you are. But oh! never put on the cloak of religion. I beseech you, do not add to your eternal misery by being a wolf in sheep's clothing. Show the cloven foot; do not hide it. If you mean to go to hell, say so. "If God be God, serve him. If Baal be God, serve him." Do not serve Baal and then pretend to be serving God.

One other practical conclusion. If God sees and knows everything, how this ought to make you tremble—you that have lived in sin for many years! I have known a man who was once stopped from an act of sin by the fact of there being a cat in the room. He could not bear even the eyes of that poor creature to see him. Oh, I wish you could carry about with you the recollection of those eyes that are always on you. Swearer! could you swear if you could see God's eyes looking at you! Thief! drunkard! harlot! could you indulge in your sins if you saw his eyes on you? Oh, I think they would startle you and bid you pause before you did in God's own sight rebel against his law. There is a story told of the American War, that one of the prisoners taken by the Americans was subjected to a torture of the most refined character. He says, "I was put into a narrow dungeon. I was comfortably provided for with all I needed. But there was a round slit in the wall, and through that, both night and day, a soldier always looked at me." He says, "I could not rest, I could not eat nor drink, nor do anything in comfort, because there was always that eye—an eye that seemed never to be turned away, and never shut—always following me around that little apartment. Nothing ever hidden from it." Now take home that figure. Recollect that is your position; you are shut in by the narrow walls of time, when you eat and when you drink, when you rise and when you lie upon your beds; when you walk the streets or when you sit at home, those eyes are always fixed upon you. Go home now and sin against God, if you dare. Go home now and break His laws to His face, despise Him, and set Him at nothing. Rush on your own destruction. Dash yourselves against the buckler of Jehovah and destroy yourselves upon His own sword! No, rather "turn ye, turn ye." Turn you that have followed the ways of sin, turn to Christ and live. Then the same Omniscience which is now your horror shall be your pleasure. Sinner! if you now pray, He sees you. If you now weep, He sees you. "When he was yet a great way off his father saw him, and ran, and fell on his neck and kissed him." It shall be even so with you, if now you turn to God and do believe in His Son Jesus Christ.

6

The Cause and Cure
of a Wounded Spirit

*The spirit of a man will sustain his infirmity; but a wounded spirit
who can bear? (Proverbs 18:14).*

Every man, sooner or later, has some kind of infirmity to bear. It
may be that his constitution from the very first will be inclined
to certain diseases and pains, or possibly he may, in passing
through life, suffer from accident or decline of health. He may not,
however, have any infirmity of the body. He may enjoy the great blessing of health, but he may have what is even worse, an infirmity of
mind. There will be something about each man's infirmity which he
would alter if he could. If he should not have any infirmity of body or
of mind, he will have a cross to carry of some kind—in his relatives, in
his business, or in certain of his circumstances. This world is not the
Garden of Eden, and you cannot make it to be so. It is like that garden
in this respect—that the serpent is in it, and the trail of the serpent is
over everything here. It is said that there is a skeleton in some closet or
other of everybody's house. I will not say so much as that; but I am
persuaded that there is no man in this world but has trial in some form
or other, unless it be those whom God permits to have their portion in
this life because they will have no portion of bliss in the life that is to
come. There are some such people who appear to have no afflictions
and trials; but as the apostle reminds us, "If ye be without chastisement, whereof all (the true seed of the Lord) are partakers, then are ye
bastards, and not sons." None of us would wish to have that terrible
name truthfully applied to us. I could greatly prefer to come into the
condition of the apostle when he said, "Most gladly therefore will I

This sermon was taken from *The Metropolitan Tabernacle Pulpit* and was
preached on Thursday evening, April 16, 1885.

74

rather, glory in my infirmities, that the power of Christ may rest upon me."

I say again, that every man will have to bear an infirmity of some sort or other. To bear that infirmity is not difficult when the spirit is sound and strong: "The spirit of a man will sustain his infirmity."

What Is That Sound Spirit
Which Will Sustain a Man's Infirmities?

Such a spirit may be found, in a minor degree, in merely natural men. Among the Stoics, there were men who bore pain and poverty and reproach without evincing the slightest feeling. Among the Romans, in their heroic days, there was one named Scoevola who thrust his right hand into the fire and suffered it to be burnt off in order to let the foreign tyrant know that there were Romans who did not care for pain. We have read wonderful stories of the patience and stern endurance of even natural men, for our text is true in that sense, "the spirit of a man will sustain his infirmity." Whatever it was that was placed upon some men, they seemed as if they carried it without a care or without a thought, so brave was their heart within them. Yet, if we knew more of these people, we should find that there were some points in which their natural strength failed them. For it must be so, the creature at its best estate is altogether vanity. David truly said, "God has spoken once; twice have I heard this: that power belongeth unto God." The strength of mind by which Christian men are able to bear their infirmities is of a higher kind than that which comes from either stoicism or from natural sternness or from obedience to any of the precepts of human philosophy.

The spirit which will best bear infirmities is, first of all, *a gracious spirit wrought in us by the Spirit of God*. If you would bear your trouble without complaining, if you would sustain your burden without fainting, if you would mount on wings as eagles, if you would run without weariness and walk without fainting, you must have the life of God within you, you must be born again, you must be in living union with Him who is the Strong One, and who, by the life which He implants within you, can give you of His own strength. I do not believe that anything but that which is divine will stand the wear and tear of this world's temptations, and of this world's trials and troubles.

> Mere mortal power shall fade and die,
> And youthful vigour cease;

but they that trust in the Lord, and derive their power from him, shall press forward even to victory. So then, first, if you would sustain your infirmity, you must have a gracious spirit, that is, a spirit renewed by grace divine.

Further, I think that a sound spirit which can sustain infirmity will be *a spirit cleansed in the precious blood of Christ.* "Conscience does make cowards of us all;" it is only when conscience is pacified by the application of the blood of sprinkling that we are able to sustain our infirmities. The restful child of God will say, "What matters it if I am consumptive? What matters it if I have a broken leg? My sin is forgiven me, and I am on my way to heaven. What matters anything else? Have you not sometimes felt that, if you had to spend the rest of your life in a dungeon, and to live on bread and water, or to lie there, as John Bunyan would have said, until the moss grew on your eyelids, yet, as long as you were sure that you were cleansed from sin by the precious blood of Christ, you could bear it all. For, after all, what are any pains and sufferings that the whips and scourges of this mortal life can lay upon us, compared with the terrors that have to be endured when sin is discerned by an awakened conscience and the wrath of God lies heavily upon us? Believe me when I say that I would rather suffer such physical pangs as may belong to hell itself than I would endure the wrath of God in my spirit. For there is nothing that can touch the very marrow of our being like a sense of divine anger when it comes upon the soul, when God seems to dip His arrows in the lake of fire, and then shoot them at us until they wound the very apple of our eye. Our whole being seems to be a mass of pain and misery. Oh, this is dreadful! But, once delivered from all fear of the righteous vengeance of God, and I can sing with Dr. Watts—

> If sin be pardon'd, I'm secure;
> Death hath no sting beside;
> The law gives sin its damning power;
> But Christ, my ransom, died.

Take sin away and give me a spirit washed in the fountain filled with blood, and I can patiently go through anything and everything, the Lord being my Helper.

The kind of spirit, then, that a man needs to sustain his infirmity, is one which has been renewed by the Holy Spirit and washed in the precious blood of Jesus.

Next, it is *a spirit which exercises itself daily unto a growing confidence in God.* The spirit that is to sustain infirmity is not a Spirit of doubt and fear and mistrust. There is no power about such a spirit as that. It is like a body without bone or sinew or muscle. Strength lies in believing. He who can trust can work, he who can trust can suffer. The spirit that can sustain a man in his infirmity is the spirit that can say, "Though he slay me, yet will I trust in him; come what may, I will not doubt my God, for his word is strong and steadfast. Although my house be not so with God, yet hath he made with me an everlasting covenant, ordered in all things and sure." O dear sirs, I am sure that, if God calls you to do business in great waters, you will want the great bower anchor with you. You will not feel safe without it. When the Lord calls you to battle with your spiritual foes, you will feel the necessity of having upon you the whole armor of God. Above all you will need to take the shield of faith, wherewith you shall be able to quench the fiery darts of the enemy.

So, beloved, our spirit must be a renewed spirit, a blood-washed spirit, and a believing spirit, if we are to sustain our infirmity.

I must also add my belief that no spirit can so well endure sickness, loss, trial, sorrow, as *a perfectly-consecrated spirit.* The man who is free from all secondary motives, who lives only for God's glory, says, if he is sick, "How can I glorify God upon my bed?" If he is in health he cries, "How can I glorify God in my vigor?" If he is rich, he asks, "How can I glorify God with the possessions which he has put under my stewardship?" If he is poor, he says, "There must be some advantage about my poverty. How can I best use it to the glory of God?" He looks to see, not how he can comfort himself, but how he can most successfully fight his Master's battles. A soldier who is in the fight must not enter into business on his own account. Paul wrote to Timothy, "No man that warreth entangleth himself with the affairs of this life; that he may please him who hath chosen him to be a soldier." The true soldier of the cross just says, "Up hill and down dale, wet or dry, in honour or dishonour, all I have to do is to lift on high the banner of my Lord, and strike down the foe; and, if needful, even lay down my own life for his sake." The perfectly-consecrated spirit will enable a man to sustain his infirmity. But a selfish spirit will weaken him, so that he will begin to complain of this and to lament that, and will not be made "strong in the Lord, and in the power of his might."

So much, then, about the sound spirit that can sustain infirmity. May the Lord give it to every one of us! How many of us have it? "Oh!" says one, "I think I am all right. I have a sane mind in a sane body." Ah! yes, but there is another part of you that needs sanity. You need spiritual health. There are times that will come to you who have nothing to depend upon but your bodily and mental vigor, and then you will find you want something more. There will come a trial that will touch you in a very tender spot, and you will cry out, "Oh! what is it that I want?" You will find that there was an unguarded place in your harness, and the arrow of the adversary has pierced you to the soul. You must be born again even for the bearing of your present infirmity. Even for struggling through this life, you must have a new heart and a right spirit, or else sometime or other you will find yourself overthrown. "If thou hast run with the footmen, and they have wearied thee, then how canst thou contend with horses? And if in the land of peace, wherein thou trustedst,

they wearied thee, then how wilt thou do in the swelling of Jordan?"
What will you do then if you have not that divinely-given spirit which
will sustain your Infirmity? When the death-sweat is on your brow, you
will need a better handkerchief than was ever made by human hands. If
the Lord your God be not at your side then to wipe the scalding tears
from your eyes, what will you do? What will you do?

What Is a Wounded Spirit?

"A wounded spirit who can bear?" It cannot bear its own infirmity,
so it becomes a load to itself. The question is not, "What can it bear?"
but, "Who can bear it?" "A wounded spirit who can bear?"

What, then, is a wounded spirit? Well, I have known some who have
talked about having a wounded spirit, but the wound has been, after all,
a very slight affair compared with the wounds that I mean. One has been
disappointed in love. That is very sad; but still it is a trial that can be
endured. We have no right to love the creature so much as to make it our
god or our idol. I have known some who have been disappointed in the
object of their ambition. In consequence, they have had a wounded
spirit. But who are you that you should not be disappointed, and what
are you that you should have everything according to your mind? Surely,
if the Lord were to deal with you according to your sins, you would have
something to bear far worse than your present disappointment. As to
those trials of which a person says, "Nobody ever suffered as I have
done, nobody was ever treated as I have been," such statements are
altogether wrong. There are many others who have passed through equal
or even greater trials. Do not, therefore, allow these things to fret you
and to destroy your peace. Be not like the Spartan boy who put the fox
into his bosom, and carried it there though it was gnawing at his flesh
and eating right into his heart. There are some people who are so unwise
as to make earthly objects their supreme delight, and those objects
become like foxes that gnaw to their soul's destruction. I will only say
this about such wounded hearts as these: there is a good deal of sin
mingled with the sorrow, and a great deal of pride, a great deal of
creature-worship and of idolatry there. Depend upon it, if you make an
idol, and God loves you, He will break it. A Quaker lady once stood up
to speak in a little meeting and all that she said was, "Verily, I perceive
that children are idols." She did not know why she said it. But there was
a mother there who had been wearing black for years after her child had
been taken away. She had never forgiven her God for what He had done.
Now this is an evil that is to be rebuked. I dare not comfort those whose
spirits are wounded in this fashion. If they carry even their mourning too
far, we must say to them, "Dear friend, is not this rebellion against God?
May not this be petulance instead of patience? May there not be very

much here which is not at all according to the mind of Christ?" We may sorrow and be grieved when we lose our loved ones, for we are men. But we must moderate our sorrow, and bow our will to the will of the Lord, for are we not also men of God?

I will not dwell further upon that point, but there are *some forms of a wounded spirit which are serious*, and yet they are not quite what I am going afterward to speak about. Some have a wounded spirit through the cruelty of men, the unkindness of children, the ingratitude of those whom they have helped, and for whom they have had such affection that they would almost have been willing to sacrifice their own lives. It is a terrible wounding when he who should have been your friend becomes your foe, and when, like your Lord, you also have your Judas Iscariot. It is not easy to bear misrepresentation and falsehood, to have your purest motives misjudged, and to be thought to be only seeking something for yourself when you have a pure desire for the good of others. This is a very painful kind of wounded spirit, but it must not be allowed to be carried too far. We should cry to God to help us bear this trial. For, after all, who are we that we should not be despised? Who are we that we should not be belied? He is the wise man who expects this kind of trial; and, expecting it, is not disappointed when it comes. "How"—asked one of a person who had lived through the terrible French Revolution when almost all notable men were put to death— "how was it that you escaped?" He answered, "I made myself of no reputation, and nobody ever spoke of me, so I escaped." And I believe that in this world the happiest lot does not belong to those of us who are always being talked about, but to those who do not know anybody, and whom nobody knows. They can steal through the world very quietly. So do not be brokenhearted if men try to wound your spirit. When, thirty years ago, they abused me to the utmost, I felt that I need not care what they said, for I could hardly do anything worse than they said I had done. When you once get used to this kind of treatment—and you may as well do so, for you will have plenty of it if you follow Christ—it will not trouble you. You will be able to bear your infirmity without being much wounded by the unkindness of men.

There are others who have been very grievously wounded by sorrow. They have had affliction upon affliction, loss after loss, bereavement after bereavement. And we ought to feel these things; indeed, it is by feeling them that we get the good out of them. Still, every Christian man should cry to God for strength to bear repeated losses and bereavements if they are his portion. He should endeavor, in the strength of God, not to succumb, whatever his trials may be. If we do yield to temptation and begin to complain of God for permitting such things to come upon us, we shall only be kicking against the pricks, and so wound ourselves all the more. Let us be submissive to the hand that wields the rod of correction, and then very soon that rod will be taken from off our backs.

There are some who have been greatly wounded, no doubt, through sickness. A wounded spirit may be the result of diseases which seriously shake the nervous system. Let us be very tender with brethren and sisters who get into that condition. I have heard some say, rather unkindly, "Sister So-and-so is so nervous, we can hardly speak in her presence." Yes, but talking like that will not help her. There are many persons who have had this trying kind of nervousness greatly aggravated by the unkindness or thoughtlessness of friends. It is a real disease; it is not imaginary. Imagination, no doubt, contributes to it and increases it; but, still, there is a reality about it. There are some forms of physical disorder in which a person lying in bed feels great pain through another person simply walking across the room. "Oh!" you say, "that is mere imagination." Well, you may think so, if you like. But if you are ever in that painful condition—as I have been many a time—I will warrant that you will not talk in that fashion again. "But we cannot take notice of such fancies," says one. I suppose that you would like to run a steam-roller across the room, just for the sake of strengthening their nerves! But if you had the spirit of Christ, you would want to walk across the room as though your feet were flakes of snow. You would not wish to cause the poor sufferer any additional pain. I beg you, never grieve those upon whom the hand of God is lying in the form of depression of spirit, but be very tender and gentle with them. You need not encourage them in their sadness. But, at the same time, let there be no roughness in dealing with them. They have many very sore places, and the hand that touches them should be soft as down.

Yet do I not wish to speak of that kind of wounded spirit alone, for that is rather the business of the physician than of the divine. Still, it well illustrates the latter part of our text, "a wounded spirit who can bear?" But this is the kind of wounded spirit I mean. *When a soul is under a deep and terrible sense of sin*—when conviction flashes into the mind with lightning swiftness and force, and the man says, "I am guilty"—when the notion of what guilt is first comes clearly home to him, and he sees that God must be as certainly just as He is good, then he discovers that he has angered infinite love, that he has provoked almighty grace, and that he has made his best Friend to be, necessarily, his most terrible Foe. A man in such a condition as that will have a wounded spirit such as none can bear. Then you may pipe to him, but he will not dance. You may try to charm him with your amusements or to please him with your oratory, but you cannot give him peace or rest. "A wounded spirit who can bear?" You know that there was one of old who said, "My soul chooseth strangling, and death rather than my life," and there was another, Judas, who actually did strangle himself under an awful sense of his guilt in betraying his Lord. Oh! I do trust that no one of you will act as he did, for that were to damn yourself irretrievably. But I do not wonder that you cry out, "Oh, that I could hide myself in the dust to escape from the terrors of a sense of divine wrath!" "A wounded spirit who can bear?"

Sometimes, the spirit is wounded *by the fierce temptations of Satan.* I hope that you do not all understand what this means, but there are some who do. Satan tempts them to doubt, tempts them to sin, tempts them to blasphemy. Some dear friends whom I know, who are among the purest-minded of mortals, and whose lives are models of everything that is devout and right, are worried by the great adversary born morning to night, scarcely ever waking in the night without some vile suggestion of Satan or some horrible howling in their ears, "You are lost; you are lost; you are shut out from mercy forever. They are tempted even to curse God and die. That temptation brings a wounded spirit, such as they scarcely know how to bear. Who can bear it? God save you born it, if you have fallen under its terrible power!

A wounded spirit may also come through *desertion by God.* The believer has not walked carefully, he has fallen into sin and God has hidden His face from him. Ah, my friends, whenever you trifle with sin, I wish you could feel as some of God's true people have done when they have been restored after a great fall! A burnt child dreads the fire, and so does a true child of God who has ever played with sin. He has been brought back to his Lord, but he has gone the rest of his life with an aching heart and limping limbs. Many a time, in wintry weather, he has felt that his broken bones start and cry out against him with the memory of his past sins. "Deliver me," says David, "from the sins of my youth." So may some of God's best servants say in their old age. Some who once were very bright stars, but who have been for a while eclipsed, will never be able to escape from a certain sense of darkness which is still upon them. "I shall go softly all my years in the bitterness of my soul," may he say who has once grievously sinned against God after light and knowledge. Therefore, beloved, be very careful that you do not backslide. For if you do, you will have a wounded spirit which you will not know how to bear.

I believe, however, that some of God's children have a wounded spirit entirely through mistake. I am always afraid of those who get certain wild notions into their heads, ideas that are not true, I mean. They are very happy while they hold those high notions, and they look down with contempt upon others of God's people who do not go kite flying or balloon sailing as they do. I think to myself, sometimes—how will they come down when their precious balloon bursts? I have often wished them well down on the level again. I have seen them believe this and believe that which they were not warranted by the Scriptures to believe. They have affected exalted ideas of their own attainments. Their position was something wonderful. They were far up in the sky, looking down upon all the saints below! Yes, dear friends, that is all very pretty and very fine, undoubtedly; but when you come down again, then you will begin to condemn yourself for things that you need not condemn. You will be distressed and miserable in your spirit because of a disappointment which you need never have had if you had walked humbly with your God. For my own part, I can truly say that none of the novelties of this present evil age have any sort of charm for me. I am content still to abide in the old way, myself ever a poor, needy, helpless sinner, finding everything I need in Christ. If you ever hear me beginning to talk about what a fine fellow I am and how perfect I am getting, you just say, "He's off his head." Please put me in an asylum directly, for I must have lost my reason before I could have believed this modern nonsense. I feel sure that I, for one, shall not suffer any disappointment in this direction, for I shall keep just where Jack the huckster kept, and say with him—

> I'm a poor sinner, and nothing at all,
> But Jesus Christ is my all in all.

Yet I am very fearful for others, for whom there awaits a terrible time of bondage when they once come back to the place where it would have been better for them to have stopped. If I were to set up to be a prince of the realm and begin to spend at the rate of fifty thousand pounds a year, I am afraid that, in a very few days, I should have the sheriff's officer down upon me. I should not be able to pay a penny in the pound of my debts. I think I would much rather go on in my own quiet way and keep within my own means, than do anything of that kind. There are, nowadays, many spiritual spendthrifts who are pretending to spend money that does not exist. They will very soon find a sense of their poverty forced upon them, and their want will come like an armed man, demanding their surrender.

So much, then, upon the words, "a wounded spirit who can bear?"

How Are We to Avoid a Wounded Spirit So Far As It Is Evil?

I answer, first, if you are happy in the Lord, and full of joy and confidence, avoid a wounded spirit *by never offending your conscience.* Labor with all your might to be true to the light that God has given you, to be true to your understanding of God's Word, and to follow the Lord with all your heart. When Mr. Bunyan describes Christian as meeting with Apollyon in the Valley of Humiliation, and fighting that terrible battle which he so graphically describes, he tells us that the pilgrim remembered then some of the slips that he had made when he was going down into the valley. While he was fighting with Apollyon, he was remembering in his own heart the slips that he had previously made. Nothing will come to you in a time of sorrow and pain and brokenness of spirit, so sharply as a sense of sins of omission or sins of commission. When the light of God's presence is gone from you, you will begin sadly to say, "Why did I do this? Why did I not do that?" Therefore, dear friends, endeavor as much as lieth in you so to live in the time of your joy that, if there ever should come times of depression, you may not have to remember neglected duties or willful wickedness.

Again, if you would avoid a wounded spirit, *get a clear view of the Gospel.* There are numbers of Christian people who have seen the Gospel just as that half-opened eye of the blind man saw "men as trees walking." They do not yet know the difference between the covenant of works and the covenant of grace. They do not know how a Christian stands in Christ. Get them to spell that glorious word grace, if they can. Ask them to say it like this, *"free* grace." They will probably say to you, "Oh! *free* grace—that is tautology." Never mind; give it to them, tautology or not. Spell it in your own soul—free, rich, sovereign grace. Know that you, a guilty, lost sinner, are saved as a sinner, that Jesus Christ came into the world to save sinners, that in due time He died for the ungodly, and that your standing is not in yourself or in your own attainments, but wholly and entirely in the finished work of the Lord Jesus Christ. It will often prevent your getting a wounded spirit if you understand the difference between things that do really differ, and do not mix them up as so many do.

Again, you will avoid a wounded spirit *by living very near to God.* The sheep that gets bitten by the wolf is the one that does not keep near the shepherd. Ah! and I have known sheep to get bitten by the dog, and the dog did not mean them any harm though he did bite them. It has often happened that, when I have been preaching, there has been somebody dreadfully hurt. Yes, even the Good Shepherd's dog bites sometimes. But if you had kept near the Shepherd, His dog would not have bitten you, for neither the dog nor the wolf will bite those that are near Him. Let your cry be—

Oh, for a closer walk with God!

Then will come "a calm and heavenly frame." But if you get away from holy living and close communion with God, you may expect to get a wounded spirit.

So much, then, for the prevention which is better than a cure. God help us all to make good use of it!

How Is Our Spirit to Be Healed Once Wounded?

Do you need that I should tell you that *there is only One who can heal a wounded spirit?* "By his stripes we are healed." If you would be healed of the bleeding wounds of your heart, flee away to Christ. You did so once; do it again. Come to Christ now, though you may have come to Him a hundred times before. Come now just as you are, without one plea, but that His blood was shed for you. Come to Him. There is no peace for a soul that does not do this, and you must have peace if you will but come simply as you are and trust yourself with Christ.

If, however, your wounded spirit should not get peace at once, *try to remove any mistakes which may be causing you unnecessary sorrow.* Study your Bible more. Listen to plain preaching of the Gospel. Let this be to you the mark of true Gospel preaching—where Christ is everything, and the creature is nothing; where it is salvation all of grace, through the work of the Holy Spirit applying to the soul the precious blood of Jesus. Try to get a clear view of the Gospel, and many a doubt and fear will fly away when knowledge takes the place of ignorance.

Endeavor also to *get a clear view of your own trouble.* We are never frightened so much by what we know as by what we do not know. The boy thinks, as he sees something white, "That is a ghost," and that is why he is frightened. He does not know what a ghost is. He supposes that it is something mysterious, and he is superstitious, so he is frightened by the object before him. If he would go right up to it, he would see that it is a cow, and he would not be frightened any more. Half the fears in the world have no real ground. If we could but induce troubled persons dispassionately to look at their fears, their fears would vanish. Write it down in black and white if you can, and let some friend read it. Perhaps if you read it yourself, you will laugh at it. I believe that, oftentimes, with regard to the most grievous afflictions that we have in our mind, if they fretted somebody else, we should say, "I cannot think how that person can be so stupid." We almost know that we are ourselves stupid, but we do not like to confess it. I would therefore urge the wounded spirit to look at its wound. It is of no use to cover it over and to say, "Oh, it is an awful wound!" Perhaps, if you would just have it thoroughly examined, the surgeon would say to you, "Oh, it is only a flesh wound. It will soon be all right again!" And so, your drooping spirits would revive, and your wounded self would begin to heal.

One thing, however, I would say to one who has a really wounded heart is *remember Christ's sympathy with you.* O you who are tossed with tempest and not comforted, your Lord's vessel is in the storm with you! Yes, He is in the vessel with you. There is not a pang that rends the believer's heart but He has felt it first. He drinks out of the cup with you. Is it very bitter? He has had a cup full of it for every drop that you taste. This ought to comfort you. I know of no better remedy for the heart's trouble in a Christian than to feel, "My Master Himself takes no better portion than that which He gives to me."

Also let me recommend, as a choice remedy for a wounded spirit, *an enlarged view of the love of God.* I wish that some of you who have a wounded spirit would give God credit for being as kind as you are yourself. You would not suffer your child to endure a needless pain if you could remove it; neither does God afflict willingly or grieve the children of men. He would not allow you to be cast down, but would cheer and comfort you, if it was good for you. His delight is that you should be happy and joyful. Do not think that you may not take the comfort which He has set before you in His Word. He has put it there on purpose for you. Dare to take it and think well of God, and it shall be well with your soul.

If this should not cure the evil, *remember the great brevity of all your afflictions, after all.* What if you should be a child of God who has even to go to bed in the dark? You will wake up in the eternal daylight. What if, for the time being, you are in heaviness? There is a needs-be that you should be in heaviness through manifold temptation, and you will come out of it. You are not the first child of God who has been depressed or troubled. Aye, among the noblest men and women who ever lived, there has been much of this kind of thing. I noticed in the life of Sir Isaac Newton—probably the greatest mind that God ever made apart from His own dear Son—the great Sir Isaac Newton, the master and teacher of the truest philosophy, during the middle part of his life was in great distress and deep depression. Robert Boyle again, whose name is well known to those who read works of depth of thought, at one time said that he counted life to be a very heavy burden to him. And there was that sweet, charming spirit of the poet Cowper. You all know that, throughout his life, he was like a flower that blooms in the shade; yet he exhaled the sweetest perfume of holy piety and poetry. Do not, therefore, think that you are quite alone in your sorrow. Bow your head and bear it, if it cannot be removed. For but a little while and every cloud shall be swept away, and you, in the cloudless sunlight, shall behold your God. Meanwhile, His strength is sufficient for you. He will not suffer you to be tempted above what you are able to bear. If you cannot bear your infirmity because of your wounded spirit, He will bear for you both yourself and your infirmity. "O rest in the Lord, and wait patiently for him." "Let not your heart be troubled, ye believe in God, believe also in your Christ." Go away, you Hannah of a sorrowful spirit, and be no more sad. The Lord grant His comforts to you, for His Son Jesus Christ's sake! Amen.

7

A Faithful Friend

There is a friend that sticketh closer than a brother (Proverbs 18:24).

Cicero has well said, "Friendship is the only thing in the world concerning the usefulness of which all mankind are agreed." Friendship seems as necessary an element of a comfortable existence in this world as fire or water or even air itself. A man may drag along a miserable existence in proud solitary dignity, but his life is scarce life, it is nothing but an existence, the tree of being stripped of the leaves and the fruits of joy. He who would be happy here must have friends. He who would be happy hereafter must, above all things, find a friend in the world to come, in the person of God, the Father of His people.

Friendship, however, though very pleasing and exceedingly blessed, has been the cause of the greatest misery to men when it has been unworthy and unfaithful. For just in proportion as a good friend is sweet, a false friend is full of bitterness. "A faithless friend is sharper than an adder's tooth." It is sweet to repose in someone. But oh! how bitter to have that support snapped and to receive a grievous fall as the effect of your confidence. Fidelity is an absolute necessary in a true friend. We cannot rejoice in men unless they will stand faithful to us. Solomon declares that "there is a friend that sticketh closer than a brother." That friend, I suppose, he never found in the pomps and vanities of the world. He had tried them all, but he found them empty. He passed through all their joys, but he found them "vanity of vanities." Poor Savage spoke from sad experience when he said—

> You'll find the friendship of the world a show!
> Mere outward show! 'Tis like the harlot's tears,

This sermon was taken from *The New Park Street Pulpit* and was preached on Sunday morning, March 8, 1857.

86

The statesman's promise, or false patriot's zeal,
Full of fair seeming, but delusion all.

And for the most part they are. The world's friendship is ever brittle. Trust to it and you have trusted a robber; rely upon it, and you have leaned upon a thorn; aye, worse than that, upon a spear which shall pierce you to the soul with agony. Yet Solomon says he had found "a friend that sticketh closer than a brother." Not in the haunts of his unbridled pleasures, nor in the wanderings of his unlimited researches, but in the pavilion of the Most High, the secret dwelling-place of God, in the person of Jesus, the Son of God, the Friend of sinners.

It is saying a great thing to affirm that "there is a friend that sticketh closer than a brother," for the love of brotherhood has produced most valiant deeds. We have read stories of what brotherhood could do which, we think, could hardly be excelled in all the annals of friendship. Timoleon, with his shield, stood over the body of his slain brother to defend him from the insults of the foe. It was reckoned a brave deed of brotherhood that he should dare the spears of an army in defense of his brother's corpse. And many such instances have there been, in ancient and modern warfare, of the attachment of brethren.

There is a story told of two brothers in a Highland regiment who, while marching through the Highlands, lost their way. They were overtaken by one of the terrible storms which will sometimes come upon travelers unawares. Blinded by the snow, they lost their way upon the mountains. Well near frozen to death, it was with difficulty they could continue their march. One man after another dropped into the snow and disappeared. There were two brothers, however, of the name of Forsythe. One of them fell prostrate on the earth and would have lain there to die, but his brother, though barely able to drag his own limbs across the white desert, took him on his back and carried him along. As others fell one by one, this brave, true-hearted brother carried his loved one on his back until at last he himself fell down overcome with fatigue and died. His brother, however, had received such warmth from his body that he was enabled to reach the end of his journey in safety and so lived.

Here we have an instance of one brother sacrificing his life for another. I hope there are some brothers here who would be prepared to do the same if they should ever be brought into the same difficulty. It is saying a great thing to declare that "there is a friend that sticketh closer than a brother." It is putting that friend first of all in the list of loving ones. For surely, next to a mother's love, there is, and there ought to be, no higher affection in the world than the love of a brother to one begotten of the same father and dandled on the same knee. Those who have "grown in beauty side by side, and filled one house with glee," ought to love one another. And we think there have been many glorious instances and mighty proofs of the love of brethren. Yet, says Solomon, "there is a friend that sticketh closer than a brother."

To repeat our assertion, we believe that this friend is the blessed Redeemer, Jesus Christ. It shall be ours first, *to prove,* this morning, *the fact* that He sticks closer than a brother. Then as briefly as we can, to show you *why* He sticks closer than a brother. Then to finish up by giving you *some lessons that may be drawn from the doctrine* that Jesus Christ is a faithful friend.

Christ Is a Friend That Sticketh Closer Than a Brother

And in order to prove this from facts, we appeal to such of you as have had Him for a friend. Will you not, each of you, at once give your verdict that this is neither more nor less than an unexaggerated truth? He loved you before all worlds, long before the day star flung his ray across the darkness, before the wings of angels had flapped the unnavigated ether, before any of creation had struggled from the womb of nothingness, God, even our God, had set His heart upon all His children. Since that time, has He once swerved, has He once turned aside, once changed? No! You who have tasted of His love and know His grace will bear me witness that He has been a certain friend in uncertain circumstances.

> He, near your side hath always stood,
> His loving kindness, oh! how good!

You fell in Adam. Did He cease to love you? No! He became the second Adam to redeem you. You sinned in practice and brought upon your head the condemnation of God. You deserved His wrath and His utter anger. Did He then forsake you? No!

> He saw you ruined in the fall,
> Yet lov'd you notwithstanding all.

He sent His minister after you—you despised him. He preached the Gospel in your ears—you laughed at him. You broke God's Sabbath, you despised His Word. Did He then forsake you? No!

> Determined to save, he watched o'er your path,
> Whilst Satan's blind slave, you sported with death.

And at last He arrested you by His grace. He humbled you, He made you penitent, He brought you to His feet and He forgave all your sins. Since then, has He left you? You have often left Him. Has He ever left you? You have had many trials and troubles. Has He ever deserted you?

Has He ever turned away His heart and shut up His bowels of compassion? No, children of God. It is your solemn duty to say "No" and bear witness to His faithfulness. You have been in severe afflictions and in dangerous circumstances. Did your friend desert you then? Others have been faithless to you. He that eats bread with you has lifted up his heel against you. But has Christ ever forsaken you? Has there ever been a moment when you could go to Him and say, "Master, You have betrayed me." Could you once in the blackest hour of your grief dare to impugn His fidelity? Could you dare to say of Him, "Lord, You have promised what You did not perform?" Will you not bear witness now: "Not one good thing has failed of all that the Lord God has promised; all has come to pass"? And do you fear He will yet forsake you? Ask, then, the bright ones before the throne—"Ye glorified spirits! Did Christ forsake you? You have passed through Jordan's stream. Did He leave you there? You have been baptized in the black flood of death. Did He there forsake you? You have stood before the throne of God. Did He then deny you?" And they answer "No; through all the troubles of our life, in all the bitterness of death, in all the agonies of our expiring moments, and in all terrors of God's judgment, He has been with us, 'a friend that sticketh closer than a brother.'" Out of all the millions of God's redeemed, there is not one He has forsaken. Poor they have been, mean and distressed, but He has never abhorred their prayer, never turned aside from doing them good. He has been ever with them.

> For his mercy shall endure,
> Ever faithful, ever sure.

But I shall not longer stay, since I cannot prove this to the ungodly, and to the godly it is already proven, for they know it by experience. Therefore it is but little necessary that I should do more than just certify the fact that Christ is a faithful friend—a friend in every hour of need and every time of distress.

Why We May Depend
Upon Christ As a Faithful Friend

There are some things in Himself which render it certain that He will stick close to His people.

True friendship can only be made between true men whose hearts are the soul of honor. There can be no lasting friendship between bad men. Bad men may pretend to love each other, but their friendship is a rope of sand which shall be broken at any convenient season. But if a man have a sincere heart within him, and be true and noble, then we may confide in him. Spenser sings in fine old English verse—

> Ne, certes can that friendship long endure,
> However gay and goodly be the style,
> That doth in cause or evil end enure,
> For Vertue is the band that bindeth Harts most sure.

But who can find a stain in the character of Jesus or who can tarnish His honor? Has there ever been a spot on His escutcheon? Has His flag ever been trampled in the dust? Does He not stand the true witness in heaven, the faithful and just? Is it not declared of Him that He is God who cannot lie? Have we not found Him so up to this moment. May we not, knowing that He is "Holy, holy, holy Lord," confide in Him that He will stick closer to us than a brother? His goodness is the guarantee of His fidelity. He cannot fail us.

Faithfulness to us in our faults is a certain sign of fidelity in a friend. You may depend upon that man who will tell you of your faults in a kind and considerate manner. Fawning hypocrites, insidious flatterers, are the sweepings and offal of friendship. They are but the parasites upon that noble tree. But true friends put enough trust in you to tell you openly of your faults. Give me for a friend the man who will speak honestly of me before my face. Give me a friend who will not tell first one neighbor and then another, but who will come straight to my house and say, "Sir, I feel there is such-and-such a thing in you which, as my brother, I must tell you of"—that man is a true friend. He has proved himself to be so. We never get any praise for telling people of their faults, we rather hazard their dislike. A man will sometimes thank you for it, but he does not often like you any the better. Praise is a thing we all love. I met with a man the other day who said he was impervious to flattery. I was walking with him at the time, and turning around rather sharply, I said, "At any rate sir, you seem to have a high gift in flattering yourself, for you are really doing so in saying you are impervious to flattery." "You cannot flatter me," he said. I replied, "I can, if I like to try. Perhaps I may do so before the day is out." I found I could not flatter him directly, so I began by saying what a fine child that was of his. He drank it in as a precious draught. When I praised this thing and that belonging to him, I could see that he was very easily flattered—not directly, but indirectly. We are all pervious to flattery. We like the soothing cordial, only it must not be labeled flattery. We have a religious abhorrence of flattery if it be so called. Call it by any other name and we drink it in, even as the ox drinks in water. Now, child of God, has Christ ever flattered you? Has He not told you of your faults right truly? Has He not pricked your conscience even upon what you thought to gloss over—your little secret sins? Has He not provoked conscience to thunder in your ears notes of terror because of your misdeeds? Well, then, you may trust Him, for He shows that faithfulness which renders a man right trustworthy. Thus I have pointed out to you that there are reasons in Himself for which we may trust Him.

In the next place, *there are some things in His friendship which render us sure of not being deceived when we put our confidence in Him.* True friendship must not be of hasty growth. As quaint old Master Fuller says, "Let friendship creep gently to a height; if it rush to it, it may soon run itself out of breath." It is even so. I think it was Joanna Baillie said—

> Friendship is no plant of hasty growth.
> Though planted in esteem's deep fixed soil,
> The gradual culture of kind intercourse
> Must bring it to perfection.

In vain you trust the gourd over your head, O Jonah. It will not be of much use to you. It came up in a night, it may wither in a night. It is the strong stiff oak of ages growth which shall abide the tempest; which shall alike put out its wings to shield you from the sun and shall afterward find you a hovel in its heart, if necessary, in its gray old age, when its branches tremble in the blast. Friendship is true when it begins, but we must have a man's friendship long before we can say of him that he will stick closer than a brother. And how long has Christ loved you? That you cannot tell. When the ages were not born He loved you. When this world was an infant, wrapped in the swaddling clothes of mist, He loved you. When the old pyramids had not begun to be built, His heart was set upon you. Ever since you have been born He has had a strong affection for you. He looked on you in your cradle, and He loved you then. He was affianced to you when you were an infant of a span long, and He has loved you ever since. Some of you I see with gray hairs, some with heads all bald with age. He has loved you up until now and will He now forsake you? Oh! no, His friendship is so old that it must last. It has been matured by so many tempests, it has been rooted by so many winds of trouble, that it cannot but endure. It must stand. Even as the granite peak of the mountain shall not be melted because, unlike the young snow, it has braved the blast and borne the heat of the burning sun. It has stood out always, catching in its face every blow from the fist of nature, and yet been unmoved and uninjured. It shall last, for it has lasted. But when the elements shall melt, and in a stream of dissolving fire shall run away, then shall Christ's friendship still exist, for it is of older growth than they. He must be "a friend that sticketh closer than a brother." His friendship is a hoary friendship—hoary as His own head of which it is said, "His head and his hair are white like snow, as white as wool."

But note, further, *the friendship which will last does not take its rise in the chambers of mirth, nor is it fed and fattened there.* Young lady, you speak of a dear friend whom you acquired last night in a ballroom. Do not, I beseech you, misuse the word. He is not a friend if He was acquired merely there. Friends are better things than those which grow in the hot-house of pleasure. Friendship is a more lasting plant than those. You have a friend, have you? Yes; and he keeps a pair of horses and has a good establishment. Ah! but your best way to prove your friend is to know that he will be your friend when you have not so much as a mean cottage; and when houseless and without clothing, you are driven to beg your bread. Thus you would make true proof of a friend. Give me a friend who was born in the winter time, whose cradle was rocked in the storm, he will last. Our fair-weather friends shall flee away from us. I had rather have a robin for a friend than a swallow. A swallow abides with us only in the summer time, but a robin comes to us in the winter. Those are tight friends that will come the nearest to us when we are in the most distress. But those are not friends who speed themselves away when ill times come.

Believer, have you reason to fear that Christ will leave you now? Has He not been with you in the house of mourning? You found your friend where men find pearls, "In caverns deep, where darkness dwells." You found Jesus in your hour of trouble. It was on the bed of sickness that you first learned the value of His name. It was in the hour of mental anguish that you first did lay hold of the hem of His garment. Since then, your nearest and sweetest relationship has been held with Him in hours of darkness. Well then, such a friend, proved in the house of sorrow—a friend who gave his heart's blood for you, and let his soul run out in one great river of gore—such a friend never can and never will forsake you. He sticks closer than a brother.

Again, *a friend who is acquired by folly is never a lasting friend.* Do a foolish thing and make a man your friend; 'tis but a confederacy in vice, and you will soon discover that his friendship is worthless. The friendships you acquire by doing wrong, you had better be without. Oh! how many silly friendships there are springing up, the mere fruit of a sentimentalism, having no root whatever, but like the plant of which our Savior tells us, "It sprang up because it had no depth of earth." Jesus Christ's friendship is not like that. There is no ingredient of folly in it. He loves us discreetly, not winking or conniving at our follies, but instilling into us His wisdom. His love is wise. He has chosen us according to the counsel of His wisdom, not blindly and rashly, but with all judgment and prudence.

Under this head I may likewise observe that *the friendship of ignorance is not a very desirable one.* I desire no man to call himself my friend if he does not know me. Let him love me in proportion to his knowledge of me. If he loves me for the little he knows, when he knows more he may cast me aside. "That man," says one, "seems to be a very amiable man." "I am sure I can love him," says another, as he scans his features. Aye, but do not write "friend" yet; wait a wee bit, until you know more of him. Just see him, examine him, try him, test him, and not until then enter him on the sacred list of friends. Be friendly to all, but make none your friends until they know you and you know them. Many a friendship born in the darkness of ignorance has died suddenly in the light of a better acquaintance with each other. You supposed men to be different from what they were, and when you discovered their real character you disregarded them. I remember one saying to me, "I have great affection for you, sir." Then he proceeded to mentioned a certain reason. I replied, "My dear fellow, your reason is absolutely false. The very thing you love me for, I am not, and hope I never shall be." And so I said, "I really cannot accept your friendship if it be founded upon a misunderstanding of what I may have said." But our Lord Jesus never can forsake those whom once He loves because He can discover nothing in us worse than He knew, for he knew all about us beforehand. He saw our leprosy, and yet He loved us. He knew our deceitfulness and unbelief, and yet He did press us to His bosom. He knew what poor fools we were, and yet He said He would never leave us nor forsake us. He knew that we would rebel against Him and despise His counsel often times. He knew that even when we loved Him, our love would be cold and languid; but He loved for His own sake. Surely, then, He will stick closer than a brother.

Yet again, *friendship and love, to be real, must not lie in words but in deeds.* The friendship of bare compliment is the fashion of this age because this age is the age of deceit. The world is the great house of sham. Go where you may in London, sham is staring you in the face; there are very few real things to be discovered. I allude not merely to tricks in business, adulterations in food, and such like deception is not confined to the tradesman's shop. It prevails throughout society; the sanctuary is not exempt. The preacher adopts a sham voice. You hardly ever hear a man speak in the pulpit in the same way he would speak in the parlor. Why, I hear my brethren, sometimes, when they are at tea or dinner speak in a very comfortable, decent sort of polished voice, but when they get into their pulpits they adopt a sanctimonious tone and fill their mouths with inflated utterance or else whine most pitifully. They degrade the pulpit by pretending to honor it—speaking in a voice which God never intended any mortal to have. This is the great house of sham; such little things show which way the wind blows. You leave your card at a friend's house. That is an act of friendship—the card! I wonder whether, if he were hard up for cash, you would leave your banker's book! You write, "My dear sir," "Yours very truly." It is a sham; you do not mean it. "Dear!" that is a sacred word. It ought to be used to none but those you regard with affection. But we tolerate falsehoods now as if they were truths, and we call them courtesies. Courtesies they may be; but untruths they are in many cases. Now, Christ's love lies not in words but in deeds. He says not, "My dear people"; but He let His heart out, and we could see what that was. He does not come to us and say, "Dearly beloved" simply. But He hangs upon the cross, and there we read "Dearly beloved" in red letters. He does not come to us with the kisses of His lips first—He gives us blessings with both His hands. He gives Himself *for* us, and then He gives Himself *to* us. Trust no complimentary friend. Rely upon the man who gives you real tokens worth your having, who does for you deeds to show the truthfulness of His heart. Such a friend—and such is Jesus—"sticketh closer than a brother."

Once more and I shall not weary you, I trust. *A purchased friend will never last long.* Give to a man nineteen times and deny him the twentieth, and he shall hate you. For his love sprang only from your gifts. The love which could buy for gold I would sell for dross. The friendship that I could buy for pearls I would dispense with for pebbles. It were of no value, and therefore the sooner lost the better. But oh! believer, Christ's love was unpurchased love. You brought Him no present. Jacob said, when his sons went to Egypt, "Take the man a present, a little oil, a little balm, a few nuts and almonds." But you took Christ no presents. When you came to Him you said—

> Nothing in my hands I bring,
> Simply to thy cross I cling.

You did not even promise that you would love Him. You had such a faithless heart, you dare not say so. You asked Him to make you love Him, that was the most you could do. He loved you for nothing at all—simply because He would love you. Well, that love which so lived on nothing but its own resources will not starve through the scantiness of your returns. The love which grew in such a rocky heart as this will not die for want of soil. That love which sprang up in the barren desert, in your unirrigated soul, will never, never die for want of moisture. It must live, it cannot expire. Jesus must be "a friend that sticketh closer than a brother."

Shall I stay to urge more reasons? I may but mention one other, namely, this—that *there cannot, by any possibility, arise any cause which could make Christ love us less.* You say, how is this? One man loves his friend, but he on a sudden grows rich. Now he says, I am a greater man than I used to be. I forget my old acquaintances. But Christ can grow no richer. He is as rich as He can be, infinitely so. He loves you now. Then it cannot be possible that He will by reason of an increase in His own personal glory forsake you, for everlasting glories now crown His head. He can never be more glorious and great, and therefore He will love you still. Sometimes, on the other hand, one friend grows poorer, and then the other forsakes him. But you never can grow poorer than you are, for you are "a poor sinner and nothing at all" now. You have nothing of your own, all you have is borrowed, all given you by Him. He cannot love you, then, less because you grow poorer, for poverty that has nothing is at least as poor as it can be and can never sink lower in the scale. Christ, therefore, must love you for all your nakedness and all your poverty.

"But I may prove sinful," says you. Yes, but you cannot be more so than He foreknew you would be. Yet He loved you with the foreknowledge of all your sins. Surely then, when it happens it will occasion no surprise to Him. He knew it all beforehand, and He cannot swerve from His love. No circumstance can possibly arise that ever will divide the Savior from His love to His people, and the saint from his love to his Savior. He is "a friend that sticketh closer than a brother."

An Inference to Be Derived From This

Lavater says, "The qualities of your friends will be those of your enemies: cold friends, cold enemies; half friends, half enemies; fervid enemies, warm friends." Knowing this to be a truth, I have often congratulated myself when my enemies have spoken fiercely against me. Well, I have thought, "My friends love me hard and fast, let the enemies be as hot as they please. It only indicates that the friends are proportionately firm in affection." Then we draw this inference, that if Christ sticks close and He is our friend, then our enemies will stick close, and never leave us until we die. Oh, Christian, because Christ sticks close, the Devil will stick too. He will be at you and with you. The dog of hell will never cease his howlings, until you reach the other side of Jordan. No place in this world is out of bow-shot of that great enemy, until you have crossed the stream his arrows *can* reach you, and they will. If Christ gave Himself for you, the Devil will do all he can to destroy you. If Christ has been longsuffering to you, Satan will be persevering in hopes that Christ may forget you. He will strive after you, and strive until he shall see you safely landed in heaven. But be not disappointed, the louder Satan roars, the more proof you shall have of Christ's love. "Give me," said old Rutherford, "give me a roaring devil rather than a sleeping one. For sleeping devils make me slumber, but roaring ones provoke me to run to my Master." Oh! be glad then, if the

world rant at you, if your foes attack you fiercely. Christ is just as full
of love to you as they are of hatred. Therefore,

> Be firm and strong;
> Be grace thy shield, and Christ thy song.

And now I have a question to ask. That question I ask of every man
and every woman in this place, and of every child too: Is Jesus Christ
your friend? Have you a friend at court—at heaven's court? Is the
Judge of quick and dead your friend? Can you say that you love Him,
and has He ever revealed Himself in the way of love to you? Dear
hearer, do not answer that question for your neighbor, answer it for
yourself. Peer or peasant, rich or poor, learned or illiterate, this question
is for each of you; therefore, ask it. Is Christ my friend? Did you ever
consider that question? Have you ever asked it? Oh! to be able to say
"Christ is my friend," is one of the sweetest things in the world. A man
who had lived much in sin one day casually entered a place of worship.
Before the sermon, this hymn was sung—

> Jesus, Lover of My Soul.

The next day the man was met by an acquaintance who asked him
how he liked the sermon. Said he, "I do not know, but there were two or
three words that took such a hold of me that I did not know what to do
with myself. The minister read that hymn, 'Jesus, Lover of My Soul.'
Ah!" said he, though he was by no means a religious man, "to be able
to say that, I would give up all I have got! But do you think," he asked,
"that Jesus ever will be the lover of such a man as I am? 'Jesus, lover of
my soul!' Oh! could I say it." And then he buried his head in his hands
and wept. I have every reason to fear that he went back to his sin and
was the same afterward as before. But you see, he had conscience
enough to let him know how valuable it was to have Christ for his lover
and his friend.

Ah! rich man, you have many friends. There be some here who have
learned the faithlessness of friends. There be some here who have toiled
for their country's good and deserve a meed of honor at their country's
hands, who, for one mistake—or what perhaps was a mistake—have
been neglected by too many who once appeared to be their most trusty
adherents. Oh! put no confidence, you great men and you rich, in the
adherence of your friends. David said in his haste, "All men are liars."
You may one day have to say it at your leisure. And oh! you kind and
affectionate hearts who are not rich in wealth, but who are rich in
love—and that is the world's best wealth—put this golden coin among
your silver ones, and it will sanctify them all. Get Christ's love shed
abroad in your hearts, and your mother's love, your daughter's love,

your husband's love, your wife's love, will become more sweet than ever. The love of Christ casts not out the love of relatives, but it sanctifies our loves and makes them sweeter far. Remember, dear hearer, the love of men and women is very sweet, but all must pass away.

What will you do if you have no wealth but the wealth that fades, and no love but the love which dies, when death shall come? Oh! to have the love of Christ! You can take that across the river death with you. You can wear it as your bracelet in heaven and set it up as a seal upon your hand, for His love is "strong as death and mightier than the grave." Good old Bishop Beveridge, I think it was, when dying did not know his best friends. Said one, "Bishop Beveridge, do you know me?" Said he, "Who are you?" and when the name was mentioned, he said, "No." "But don't you know your wife, Bishop?" "What is her name?" said he. Said she, "I am your wife." "I did not know I had got one," said he. Poor old man! his faculties all failed him. At last one stooped down and whispered, "Do you know the Lord Jesus Christ?" "Yes," said he, making an effort to speak, "I have known Him these forty years, and I never can forget Him." It is marvelous how memory will hold the place with Jesus, when it will with no one else; and it is equally marvelous, that

> When all created streams are dry,
> Christ's fulness is the same.

My dear hearers, do think of this matter. Oh that you might get Christ for your friend. He will never be your friend while you are self-righteous; he will never be your friend while you live in sin. But do you believe yourselves guilty? Do you desire to leave off sin? Do you want to be saved? Do you desire to be renewed? Then let me tell you, my Master loves you! Poor, weak, and helpless worms, my Master's heart is full of love to you. His eyes at this moment are looking down with pity on you. "Oh! Jerusalem, Jerusalem, Jerusalem!" He now bids me tell you that He died for all of you who confess yourselves to be sinners and feel it. He bids me say to you, "Believe on the Lord Jesus Christ, and you shall be saved." He tells me to proclaim salvation full and free—full, needing nothing of yours to help it; free, needing nothing of yours to buy it.

> Come, ye thirsty, come and welcome;
> God's free bounty glorify:
> True belief and true repentance,
> Every grace that brings us nigh—
> Without money,
> Come to Jesus Christ, and buy.

There is nothing I feel that I fail so much in as addressing sinners. Oh! I wish I could cry my heart out and preach my heart out to you and at you.

> Dear Saviour, draw reluctant hearts;
>   To thee let sinners fly,
> And take the bliss thy love imparts;
>   And drink, and never die.

Farewell, with this one thought—we shall never all of us meet together here again. It is a very solemn thought, but according to the course of nature and the number of deaths, if all of you were willing to come here next Sabbath morning, it is not at all likely that all of you will be alive. One out of this congregation will be sure to have gone the way of all flesh. Farewell, you that are appointed to death. I know not where you are—yon strong man or yon tender maiden, with the hectic flush of consumption on her cheek. I know not who is appointed to death, but I do now most solemnly take my farewell of such a one. Farewell poor soul; and is it farewell forever? Shall we meet in the land of the hereafter, in the home of the blessed? Or do I bid you farewell now forever? I do solemnly bid farewell to you forever, if you live and die without Christ. But I cannot bear that dreary thought. I therefore say, poor sinner! stop and consider—consider your ways, and now "turn ye, turn ye, why will ye die?" "Why will ye *die?*" "Why will *ye* die?" "Why *will* ye die?" Ah! you cannot answer that question. May God help you to answer it in a better fashion: by saying—"Here, Lord!

> Just as I am, without one plea,
> But that thy blood was shed for me,
> O Son of God, I come to thee.

I trust my soul in thy kind hands." The Lord bless you all; for Christ's sake! Amen.

8

God's Glory in Hiding Sin

It is the glory of God to conceal a thing: but the honour of kings is to search out a matter (Proverbs 25:2).

The translation of our text, if it had been more literal, would have run thus, "It is the glory of God to cover a matter, but the honour of kings is to search out a matter." For the sake of variety in language, our translators sometimes gave two different interpretations to the same word. Though that makes the verbiage more smooth, it is generally a great mistake, and apt to mislead us. The word "conceal" is just the same word that we get in the passage, "Blessed is he . . . whose sin is covered." So the text runs thus, I will give it to you again that I may further impress it upon you. "It is the glory of God to cover a matter, but the honor of kings is to search out a matter."

First of all, I will give you the common interpretation which is given to these words, and the topic which is suggested to most minds thereby, namely, that it is God's glory to conceal much of the great truth which concerns Himself and His dealings with the sons of men. "Clouds and darkness are round about him." It is His glory that He is not seen—His glory that He is concealed. While, as for kings, it is their honor "to search out a matter." This is the general interpretation which almost every expositor gives of this passage, but I am not able wholly to agree with it. However, I will speak upon it for a little while.

It is certain that such an explanation as this would have to be taken in a limited sense, for it cannot absolutely and without qualification be the glory of God to conceal a thing. For, if so, He might have concealed everything from us. It is evidently for His glory that some things should be revealed; or, else, why has He revealed them? He might have dwelt forever in that wondrous solitude in which we suppose He did dwell

---

This sermon was taken from *The Metropolitan Tabernacle Pulpit* and was preached on Sunday evening, July 15, 1877.

before He commenced the work of creation. We know not what He was doing in that past eternity of which it is difficult, if not impossible, for us to conceive—when there was no creation, when not a single star had begun to shine, nor an angel had fled through space on rapid wing. If it were God's glory to be absolutely concealed, it seems to me that He would have remained alone in the thick darkness that surrounded Him, for He would not have wanted to have a single creature to know His love, to realize His power, or to contemplate His wisdom. It is at once obvious that, if this is the true and correct interpretation, "It is the glory of God to conceal a thing," it must be taken in a very limited sense. If it had been His glory to conceal everything, He would have continued to conceal it. But, as far as I can see, His manifested glory is His glory. The glory of God is not so much to conceal as to reveal Himself to those whom He prepares to receive the revelation.

There are many things which it would not be for God's glory to conceal. You could not say of everything, "It is the glory of God to conceal this." Take, for instance, His righteous law. Would it have been for His glory to have left our race utterly ignorant of it? I cannot conceive of such a thing! And then His matchless redemption He has revealed to us in many wonderful ways. Would He have taken all the pains that He has done to reveal Himself in Christ Jesus if it had been for His glory to conceal Himself in that respect? Would He bid us go into all the world and preach the Gospel to every creature, if it could be for His glory to conceal that? No, it is high treason against the majesty of heaven for any man to obscure the blessed revelation of God in Christ Jesus. I am afraid that all of us preachers of the Word do that, in some measure, by reason of our infirmity. But God forbid that we should ever willfully keep back a single ray of the glory of God in the face of Jesus Christ!

There are many great and glorious truths which do not need that God should conceal them. If we do not perceive them, probably it is because it is not necessary that they should be concealed, for their own inherent glory is their concealment. If I were to take, for instance, the mysterious doctrine of the eternal filiation of the Lord Jesus Christ or the procession of the Holy Spirit from the Father and the Son, these wondrous truths need not be concealed from us because they are, in themselves, such deep mysteries that, however clearly they may be revealed to us, it is not possible for us to understand them. Even the grand doctrine of the Trinity, which is so plainly set forth in the Scriptures—the Trinity in the Unity of the Godhead—need not be concealed as, indeed, it has not been, yet we cannot comprehend it. God need not seek out any method of concealment, for if He were to unveil His face among us, the glory would be too bright to be beheld. Go and stand, O mortal man, and gaze upon the sun at midday! Can you do it! Would not your eyes be thereby blinded! Yet, the sun is only one of the myriads of servants in the courts of God. Then, what must the face of the King Himself be! It needs not that He should veil it. His own glory is, surely, veil enough to itself. Our minds are finite, contracted, limited. There were certain men who called themselves "Encyclopaedists" because they fancied that they knew everything. Yet they knew nothing perfectly, and many of them broke down altogether in their attempt to learn even all that might be known by men. But, as for God Himself, who can possibly comprehend Him! The archangel, who stands nearest to His august presence, must veil his face with his wings, for even he is not able to gaze upon the glory of that excessive light. It does not seem to me to be so great a truth that it is the glory of God to conceal as that His very glory does conceal itself, not by being concealed, but by being so exceedingly unveiled. The glory itself blinds, for the finite mind of man is not able to gaze thereon.

Yet the truth, which our English Version seeks to convey to us, may be accepted without hesitation if we regard it thus: if God has concealed anything, it is God's glory to conceal it, and it is right that it should be hidden. If God has not told us any truth, it is for His glory not to tell it to us. Perhaps we have as much reason to bless the Lord for what is not in the Bible as for what is there. What He has not revealed may be as much for our benefit, and, certainly, is as much for His glory as what He has revealed. For instance, if He does not tell us all about Himself and the mystery of His person, do we want to know it? Can we not believe in Him and love Him all the better because we do not understand Him! Surely, a God whom we could understand would be no God. We delight in being out of our depth—in finding waters to swim in—where understanding, with its little plumb-line, finds no bottom, but where love, with a restful spirit, finds perfect peace. Doubtless, there is a glory in the Lord not revealing Himself so far as the past or present is concerned.

As to the future, it is, no doubt, for the glory of God that He has not revealed to us all concerning the history of this world. It may be all in the Book of Daniel and the Book of Revelation. Some friends think it is, and it may be. But this I venture to say, there is no man who understands it, and I do not think any man will understand it until the Word shall explain itself. Then possibly, when history becomes the commentary upon the prophesy, we shall wonder that we did not see it. Yet we cannot do so at present. It is to the glory of God, and to your own profiting, that you do not know what will happen to you tomorrow. You know not what afflictions may await you nor when you shall die. It is well for you that you do not know. If it had been for God's glory that you should read your history from its first page to its last, and be able to foretell every event in your own life story or in the history of the nations of the earth, God would have revealed it to you. But be content not to know what God does not tell you, and say in your spirit, "Let it be so; for, in some things it is the glory of God to conceal a thing."

Still, I think that this is not the teaching of the text. I conceive that it has quite another meaning, which I will try to give you. You know that in a proverb like this with a "but" in the middle, there is what we call an antithesis or an expression of opposites. The text does not run thus, "It is the glory of God to conceal a thing: but the honour of kings is to publish a thing." That is not what is said here. It is quite a different sentence, which is not an antithesis at all. Then, again, the antithesis is not complete, "It is the glory of God to conceal a thing: but the honour of kings is to search out a matter," for it is not so much the business of kings to search out matters that refer to wisdom as it is the business of wise men to do so. If there are doctrines that are not known to us because God conceals them, it is the business of wise men to search them out and not so much the business of kings to do so. Neither can we read the passage thus, "It is the glory of God to conceal a thing, but the honour of kings to make things plain," because the third verse of the chapter does not agree with this rendering. Solomon did not think that it was to the honor of kings to make things plain. He was a believer in diplomacy, for he says, "The heaven for height, and the earth for depth, and the heart of kings is unsearchable." He could not, therefore, have intended to convey that meaning.

Now let me give you what I think is the true meaning of the passage. What is the business of kings? Why are they set up above their fellowmen? What is their honor? Why, it is the honor of kings to search out matters that concern the administration of justice, to bring prisoners before their bar, laying bare their crimes, and convicting them if they are guilty. It is the glory of God to cover a matter, that matter being sin. But it is the honor of kings to search that matter out and bring the guilty one to justice. You know that we think less and less of our police if they are not able to discover criminals. It has sometimes happened that justice misses its mark. Perhaps there is an attempt made to get a certain important witness out of the way, or to suborn another, or to suppress some testimony that might be brought against the accused persons. It is never to the honor of kings when that is done. When, for instance, a murder has been committed, and the criminal cannot be traced, it is not to the credit of the governing powers that it should be so. Though it must be so sometimes, for no human government can be perfect in its detective forces, yet it is not to the honor of "the powers that be." It is to the honor of kings that they search matters out until they bring home the guilt to the proper individual. Nor is it to the honor of kings if they give their verdict and sentence at first sight according to prejudice. It is their honor to search out a matter—to hear both sides of the case. The magistrate, who sits in the king's name, is bound to inquire thoroughly into the matter brought before him, and at last to adjudicate as justice demands. This is sometimes very difficult, but it is to the honor of kings and their representatives when they attempt it.

Now, to God, such a thing as this is impossible. Nothing is concealed from Him. The whole universe is but one great prison for those who offend against Him, and He can find them at any time that He pleases, and He can execute His just sentence upon them without a moment's delay. He needs no witness. He need not summon this person or that who has seen a certain deed done, for the transgression has been committed in His own sight. His glory is that He covers the matter. As it is the glory of God to cover the matter, it is also the honor of kings to search the matter out—that matter, in each case, being the breach of law. I am persuaded that this is the meaning of the text. Even if it were not, it is a grand truth of Scripture well worthy of our meditation.

So, we shall dwell upon it thus. First, *it is the glory of God to cover sin.* Secondly, *this is a great encouragement to penitent sinners.* Thirdly, *it ought to be a great stimulus to saints.*

It Is the Glory of God to Cover Sin

This is the expression which is commonly used in Scripture to describe *the putting away of sin and forgiving it.* God covers the very thing which the magistrate searches out—guilt, the breach of His law, the aggravations, the multiplied repetitions of sin, the base motives, the many excuses and deceits with which sin is sought to be extenuated— all this God covers. Hear this and be astonished, O sinners, God can cover all your sins. No matter how black they are, or how many, or how deep their dye, He can cover them all!

> This is his grand prerogative,
> And none can in this honor share.

But He can do it, glory be to His blessed name!

He can cover the sin which is known and confessed. He never covers the sin which is unconfessed. When a man will not acknowledge himself to be guilty, he stands convicted of his rebellious refusal to take his proper position before the Lord. But if you do stand, O sinner, and confess your guilt—if you say, O rebel, "There is no doubt about the matter; I own that I am guilty"—it is the glory of God that He can cover that sin which no other can cover, and which your own conscience will not permit you to conceal! He can cover the transgression of that man whose mouth is stopped by the consciousness of his guilt. O glorious act of divine grace, that sin and transgression can be covered—covered, though it be confessed and acknowledged, and covered because it is confessed and acknowledged!

The glory of this truth lies in the fact that *God can do this justly through the work of Jesus.* To cover up sin—why, standing as it does, alone, and without any qualification—it might seem to be a dreadful thing for God to do, but He can do it righteously. Without the slightest violation of His law—without endangering the stability of His kingdom—he can forgive and cover up all manner of sin and blasphemy so that it shall never be seen again. Do you ask me how this can be done? The answer lies in the great substitutionary sacrifice of Jesus Christ. God steps down from His eternal throne when man must be punished for his sin, and He says, "I will bear the punishment; lay it all on Me." And that He might bear it, Jesus took upon Himself the form of a man and dwelt among men. At last, upon the accursed tree He bore the guilt of man. It was a wondrous recompense which He made to His own law by being Himself punished in the stead of the offender. Now, beneath the whole heavens, there can be none who can justly object to the covering of sin by the atoning sacrifice of Jesus Christ. That singular, that remarkable, that unique transaction of the Just suffering for the unjust, that He might bring us to God, has enabled God to cover our sin, and to do it justly.

Further, He can do this *without exacting any sort of compensation from the offender.* Marvelous is this truth—too marvelous for some to believe. The Romish Church teaches us that we must do penance if our sin is to be forgiven. There must be so many lashes for the bare back, or so long abstention from food, beside purgatorial pains to be inflicted after death, and I know not what beside. Aye, but this is the glory of God, that He can cover all this sin now, upon the spot, without any price being paid by the sinner or any suffering being endured by him. He has but to come and confess his sin, and accept the divine covering, namely, the blood and righteousness of Jesus Christ, and the whole of it shall be covered once for all.

It is the glory of God that *He can do all this without any injury to the person who is forgiven.* It sometimes happens that, if a man has offended you, and you forgive him again and again, he may thereby become hardened in his sin. But the Lord's sweet way of covering sin is one which always melts and changes the heart. Sin is never so heartily hated as when it is covered by the blood of Christ. No man does ever thoroughly loathe sin until he has seen it put away in Christ. But when he has seen Jesus put it away by His own griefs and death, then he really hates the sin that made the Redeemer mourn and nailed Him to the tree. It is the glory of God that He can cover sin in such a fashion as this, so as not to injure the offender whom He forgives.

And He can do it *without causing any injury to the rest of mankind.* There is no man who is any the worse because his fellowman is saved. The example of saved souls is never injurious. There are some, I know, who can twist the truth until they find in it an excuse for sin. But the truth that God is able to forgive the grossest sin—no, more, that He has forgiven it in the case of many and has pressed them to His bosom as His own dear children—has done no injury, but much helpful service to the morals of mankind. Go where you will, and read the story of the prodigal son—on board ship among rough sailors, or away there in the barracks among wild soldiery, or go into the worst slums of London, and read to fallen women that wondrous story of God's pardoning love—and see if it will do them any injury. You know that it will not. On the contrary, it conveys to them a message of hope which helps to lift them up from that black despair which is one of the strongest chains by which the Devil can hold lost souls in captivity. I am not at all afraid of the effect of preaching that it is the glory of God to blot out sin, for He put His Son between Himself and the sinner, as we sometimes sing,

> Christ and then the sinner see,
> Look through Jesu's wounds on me.

The greatest blessing of all is, dear friends, that *when God covers sin, He does it so effectually that it never appears anymore.* He declares that He casts it into the depths of the sea. He says that as far as the east is from the west, so far does He remove it from us. He even goes the length of saying, "The iniquity of Israel shall be sought for, and there shall be noise." So far as anything can be annihilated, that is what will happen to the Lord's people. You know that the work of the Messiah was, "to finish the transgression, and to make an end of sins, and to make reconciliation for iniquity, and to bring in everlasting righteousness." That is the work of which He said, "It is finished." Then it is finished, there is an end of it. That is the glorious way in which the Lord covers sin, and it is His peculiar glory that He is continually doing this. Kings may search out matters, and they ought to do so, or government will not be safe. But it is to the honor of God to forgive sin.

Great Encouragement to Those
Seeking Mercy at God's Hands

Beloved friend, do you wish to have your sin forgiven? Then, do not attempt to cover it yourself, for it is the glory of God to cover that matter, so do not try to rob Him of His glory. If you could have covered your sin, there would have been no need for a Redeemer. Do not attempt to excuse or extenuate your guilt, but make a clean breast of it. You are a sinner; therefore, say that you are a sinner. In all your approaches to God, seeking mercy at His hands, come in your true colors. Do not even plead your own repentance or your tears or your feelings. Plead as David did, "For thy name's sake, O Lord, pardon mine iniquity: *for if is great.*" Call your sin great, as it really is. Never try to make it out to be little. You know that if you were wounded on a battlefield, and a surgeon came where you were, you would not say to him, "Oh, I have very little the matter with me!" Oh no! I warrant you that you would cry as loudly as you could, "Doctor, do bind up my gaping wounds, lest I die." You know that, in such a case, you would make the most of it, and you would act wisely in doing so. It is never wise for a sinner to make himself out to be a little sinner. It is the glory of God to cover sin, so do not attempt to do it. I say again, lay it all bare before Him and ask Him to cover it with the atoning sacrifice of His dear Son.

Now, poor sinner, I pray the Holy Spirit to enable you to give God glory, at this moment, by believing that He can cover sin. When the conscience is thoroughly awakened, it seems impossible that sin should ever be covered. The convicted sinner says, "My sin, my sin, I always see it. Can it ever be hidden from the sight of God?" Can you not believe that God in Christ can cover your sin? Glorify God, O son, glorify God, O daughter, by believing that He can do so! Do not limit His mercy by thinking that He cannot pardon you, for He has forgiven so many that, assuredly, there is proof enough that He can pass by iniquity, transgression, and sin, and remember not the guilt of those who trust His Son. If you believe that, give glory to God now by believing that He is willing to pass by your sin. Every man is willing to do that which honors himself, and it is inconceivable that God should be reluctant to do that which glorifies Himself. So as it is for His glory to cover sin, He must be willing to cover it. Therefore, may the Holy Spirit help you now to believe that He can and will cover your sin!

There is Christ on the cross. Look to Him with the eye of faith, and take Him to be your own Savior. Christ on the cross is nothing to you until you trust in Him, but it glorifies Christ when a poor guilty sinner cries to Him, "Purge me with hyssop." You know what the use of the hyssop was. They took a bunch of it and dipped it in the blood of the sacrifice, and those who were sprinkled with it were made ceremonially clean. David prayed, "Purge *me* with hyssop, and *I* shall be clean: wash *me,* and *I* shall be whiter than snow." That is the prayer for you to present. You believe that, if God were to wash another man in the blood of Jesus, He would become whiter than snow, but can you not believe it for yourself? May the blessed Spirit take away your unbelief, dear heart! Can you not believe that He can wash you, and make you whiter than snow! He will do it in a moment if you do but trust Him, rely upon Him, and receive His dear Son to be your salvation. This is the true covering of sin. Oh, how the Hebrews loved that word "covering." Noah's ark was pitched within and without with pitch—that was its covering. So, everything under the Mosaic law had its covering. God has a way of covering sin, and covering the sinner, too, within and without, until all his sin is gone. He that believes on the Lord Jesus Christ may know at once that his transgression is forgiven, his sin is covered.

"But," someone asks, "am I to do nothing!" Nothing but believe in Him that justifies the ungodly. If you do that, you will begin to do something more directly afterward, for you will love God for having pardoned you. You will say, "I am not my own now, for I am bought with a price. Therefore, I will live to His glory." But, in order to get your sin forgiven, you have nothing to do except to—

> Cast thy deadly doing down,
> > Down at Jesu's feet;
> Stand in him, in him, alone,
> > Gloriously complete.

"He that believeth on him is not condemned." "He that believeth in him is justified from all things, from which he could not be justified by the law of Moses." Oh, what an encouragement this ought to be to all sinners who are seeking the Savior!

A Great Stimulus to the People of God

First, *it should excite you to glorify God in having covered your sin.* Do not go and talk to everybody about what you used to be before conversion as I have known some do. They will almost glory in what they were. I have more than a little hesitation about what is sometimes said by converted burglars and men of that sort. I am glad they are converted, but I wish they would not talk so much about that which is covered. Let it be covered. Still, never be backward to glorify God for having covered your sin. Speak of it with delicacy and modesty. But, if the grace of God has saved you, tell all men of it, and do not let people imagine that God has done only a small thing for you. When He saved you, it was the grandest thing He could do for you. Do you not think so! Well, then, tell the story of it.

> Tell it unto sinners, tell,
> I am—I am—out of hell.

And what is more, I never shall go there, but shall see God's face with acceptance in heaven. Tell this to sinners while you live. When you get to heaven, make the streets of glory to ring with the tidings of the almighty grace that covered all your sin.

The next thing for you Christian people to do, now you know that God can cover sin, is to *aim at the covering of the sins of your friends and neighbors by leading them to the Savior.* To see sin should always be a tearful sight to you. As soon as ever you see it breathe the prayer, "Lord, cover it." Do you live where you can hardly lie in your bed at night without hearing sounds of ribaldry and blasphemy? Then, the moment you hear them say, "Lord, cover that sin." Do you see in the streets foul transgression that makes you blush? Never see it without saying, "Lord, cover that sin." If we were in a right state of heart, this would be our habit. Every sin that we noticed in ourselves or in others—in our children, or our servants, or our neighbors, or that we read of in the newspapers—would make us pray, "Lord, cover that sin." So, always be telling others about the covering of sin by Christ's precious blood. Show them what a perfect covering it is. You know that the Lord spoke through Isaiah of "a covering which is narrower than that a man can wrap himself in it." But the atoning sacrifice of Christ is a covering which will cover all sin, and cover the sinner from head to foot. Therefore, tell others about it with all your might.

And, once more, you who have proved the power of this covering, imitate the Lord in forgetting the sins of those who repent. If ever they offend you, let that atonement which satisfied God for sin also satisfy you and say, "Though this man has offended me, I ask no atonement at his hands because Christ's atonement is to my soul the satisfaction for every sin against me as well as against God." Never harbor any resentment for a single moment, beloved. "Even as Christ forgave you, so also do ye." Do you think that Christ's blood and righteousness are not sufficient to cover those unkind words of your brother, or that ungenerous action of your son, or that slanderous speech of your neighbor? Go and put all offenses against yourself where God has put all offenses against Himself. It is a dreadful thing to hear a man talking about God having forgiven him ten thousand talents, and then to see him take his brother by the throat saying, "Pay me what thou owest." Our Lord Jesus Christ said, "If ye forgive not men their trespasses, neither will your Father forgive your trespasses." This spirit of forgiveness would keep us always in a state of love, and this is exactly what the Lord Jesus aims at. "It is the glory of God to cover a matter."

Then, do you cover matters too. I know some people who always like to be poking into any filth there is. They keep a long stick and stir it up, and they seem to be quite pleased with the sweet perfume. Let it alone, brother; let it alone. "Oh, but you do not know how they have offended me!" No, and I do not want to know. But I am quite sure that they have not offended you as much as you have offended God, and yet He has forgiven you. Then, do you forgive them. The less said, you know, in such matters, the sooner are they mended. Solomon wisely says, "Where no wood is, there the fire goeth out." Blessed are they who always act as firemen, throwing cold water upon every spark of dissension or ill-will that they see. It is the glory of God to cover it up, so do you also cover it up with the spirit of love and the mantle of gentleness. Above all, with the reflection that the precious blood of Christ, that made peace between you and God, has also made peace between you and all mankind. And now, for love of Christ, if they smite you on the one cheek, you should turn the other also. If they will have your cloak, for love of Jesus let them have your coat also, sooner than live in the spirit of perpetual contention and strife. May God enable you to act thus, for Christ's sake! Amen.

9

All the Day Long

Let not thine heart envy sinners: but be thou in the fear of the LORD
all the day long. For surely there is an end; and thine expectation
shall not be cut off (Proverbs 23:17–18).

L ast Lord's day we had for our texts two promises. I trust they
were full of comfort to the tried people of God and to souls in
the anguish of conviction. Today we will consider two precepts
that we may not seem to neglect any part of the Word of God, for the
precept is as divine as the promise. Here we have a command given of
the Holy Spirit through the wisest of men. Therefore, both on the divine
and on the human side it is most weighty. I said that Solomon was the
wisest of men, and yet he became, in practice, the most foolish. By his
folly, he gained a fresh store of experience of the saddest sort. We trust
that he turned to God with a penitent heart, and so became wiser than
ever—wiser with a second wisdom which the grace of God had given
him to consecrate his earthly wisdom. He who had been a voluptuous
prince became the wise preacher in Israel. Let us give our hearts to
know the wisdom which he taught.

The words of Solomon to his own son are not only wise, but full of
tender anxiety. They are worthy, therefore, to be set in the highest degree as to value, and to be received with heartiness as the language of
fatherly affection.

These verses are found in the Book of Proverbs. Let them pass current as proverbs in the church of God as they did in Israel of old. Let
them be "familiar in our mouths as household words." Let them be
often quoted, frequently weighed, and then carried into daily practice.
God grant that this particular text may become proverbial in this church

---

This sermon was taken from *The Metropolitan Tabernacle Pulpit* and was
preached on Sunday morning, July 22, 1890.

from this day forward. May the Holy Spirit impress it on every memory and heart! May it be embodied in all our lives!

If you will look steadily at the text you will see, first, *the prescribed course of the godly man:* "Be thou in the fear of the LORD all the day long." Secondly, you will note *the probable interruption* of that course. It occurred in those past ages, and it occurs still: "Let not thine heart envy sinners." We are often tempted to repine because the wicked prosper. The fear of the Lord within us is disturbed and injured by envious thoughts which will lead on to murmuring and to distrust of our heavenly Father unless they be speedily checked. So foolish and ignorant are we, that we lose our walk with God by fretting because of evil doers. Thirdly, we shall notice before we close *the helpful considera-tion* which may enable us to hold on our way and to cease from fretting about the proud prosperity of the ungodly: "For surely there is an end; and thine expectation shall not be cut off."

The Prescribed Course of the Believer

"Be thou in the fear of the LORD all the day long!" The fear of the Lord is a brief description for true religion. It is an inward condition be-tokening hearty submission to our heavenly Father. It consists very much in a holy reverence of God and a sacred awe of Him. This is ac-companied by a child-like trust in Him which leads to loving obedi-ence, tender submission, and lowly adoration. It is a filial fear. Not the fear which has torment, but that which goes with joy when we "rejoice with trembling."

We must, first of all, *be* in the fear of God before we can remain in it "all the day long." This can never be our condition except as the fruit of the new birth. To be in the fear of the Lord "ye must be born again." The fear of the Lord is the beginning of wisdom, and we are taught therein by the Holy Spirit, who is the sole author of all our grace. Where this fear exists, it is the token of eternal life, and it proves the abiding indwelling of the Holy Spirit. "Happy is the man that feareth alway." "The Lord taketh pleasure in them that fear him." This holy fear of the living God is the life of God showing itself in the quickened ones.

This fear, according to the text, is for all the day and for every day. The longest day is not to be too long for our reverence nor for our obe-dience. If our days are lengthened until the day of life declines into the evening of old age, still are we to be in the fear of God. Yes, as the day grows longer, our holy fear must be deeper.

This is contrary to the habit of those persons who have *a religion of show.* They are very fine, very holy, very devout when anybody looks at them. This is rather the love of human approbation than the fear of the

Lord. The Pharisee, with a halfpenny in one hand and a trumpet in the other, is a picture of the man who gives an alms only that his praises may be sounded forth. The Pharisee, standing at the corner of the street saying his prayers, is a picture of the man who never prays in secret, but is very glib in pious assemblies. "Verily, I say unto you, they have their reward." Show religion is a vain show. Do nothing to be seen of men, or you will ripen into a mere hypocrite.

Neither may we regard godliness as something off the common—an extraordinary thing. Have not *a religion of spasms*. We have heard of men and women who have been singularly excellent on one occasion, but never again. They blared out like comets, the wonders of a season, and they disappeared like comets, never to be seen again. Religion produced at high pressure for a supreme occasion is not a healthy growth. We need an ordinary, commonplace, everyday godliness which may be compared to the light of the fixed stars that shine evermore. Religion must not be thought of as something apart from daily life. It should be the most vital part of our existence. Our praying should be like our breathing, natural and constant. Our communion with God should be like our taking of food, a happy and natural privilege. Friends, it is a great pity when people draw a hard and fast line across their life, dividing it into the sacred and the secular. Say not, "This is religion, and the other is business," but sanctify all things. Our most common acts should be sanctified by the Word of God and prayer, and thus made into sacred deeds. The best of men have the least of jar or change of tone in their lives.

When the great Elijah knew that he was be taken up, what did he do? If you knew that tonight you would be carried away to heaven, you would think of something special with which to quit this earthly scene. Yet the most fitting thing to do would be to continue in your duty, as you would have done if nothing had been revealed to you. It was Elijah's business to go to the schools of the prophets and instruct the young students. He went about that business until he took his seat in the chariot of fire. He said to Elisha, "The Lord hath sent me to Bethel." When he had exhorted the Bethel students he thought of the other college and said to his attendant, "The Lord hath sent me to Jericho." He took his journey with as much composure as if he had a lifetime before him, and thus fulfilled his tutorship until the Lord sent him to Jordan, whence he went up by a whirlwind into heaven. What is there better for a man of God than to abide in his calling wherein he glorifies God? That which God has given you to do you should do. That, and nothing else, come what may. If any of you should tomorrow have a revelation that you must die, it would not be wise to go upstairs and sit down, and read, or pray, until the usual day's work was finished. Go on, good woman, and send the children to school, cook the dinner, and go about the proper business of the day. Then if you are to die you will have left no ends of life's web to ravel out. So live that your death shall not be a piece of strange metal soldered on to your life, but part and parcel of all that has gone before. "Be thou in the fear of the LORD all the day long." Living or dying we are the Lord's, and let us live as such.

Ours must never be a religion that is periodic in its flow, like certain intermittent springs which flow and ebb, and flow only to ebb again. Beware of the spirit which is in a rapture one hour and in a rage the next. Beware of serving Christ on Sunday, and Mammon on Monday. Beware of the godliness which varies with the calendar. Every Sunday morning some folks take out their godliness and touch it up while they are turning the brush around their best hat. Many women, after a fashion, put on the fear of God with their new bonnet. When the Sunday is over and their best things are put away, they have also put away their best thoughts and their best behavior. We must have a seven-days' religion or else we have none at all. Periodical godliness is perpetual hypocrisy. He that toward Jesus can be enemy and friend by turns is in truth always an enemy. We need a religion which, like the poor, we have always with us. We need a religion which, like our hearts, is always throbbing and, like our breath, is always moving. Some people have strange notions on this point. They are holy only on holy days and in holy places. There was a man who was always pious on Good Friday. He showed no token of religion on any other Friday, or indeed on any other day. But on Good Friday nothing would stop him from going to church in the morning after he had eaten a hotcross bun for breakfast. That day he took the Sacrament and felt much better. Surely he might well enough do so, since on his theory he had taken in grace enough to last him for another year. You and I believe such ideas to be ignorant and superstitious. But we must take heed that we do not err after a similar manner. Every Friday must be a Good Friday to us. May we become so truly gracious that to us every day becomes a holy day; our garments, vestments; our meals, sacraments; our houses, temples; our families, churches; our lives, sacrifices; ourselves kings and priests to God! May the bells upon our horses be "holiness unto the Lord"! God send us religion of this kind, for this will involve our being "in the fear of the LORD all the day long."

Let us practically note the details which are comprised in the exhortation, "Be thou in the fear of the LORD all the day long." The sun is up and we awake. May we each one feel, "When I awake I am still with thee." It is wise to rise in proper time. Drowsiness may waste an hour, and cause us to be behindhand all the day, so that we cannot get into order, and act as those who quietly walk with God. If I am bound to be in the fear of God all the day long, I am bound to begin well with earnest prayer and sweet communion with God. On rising, it is as essential to prepare the heart as to wash the face; as necessary to put on Christ as to put on one's garments. Our first word should be with our heavenly Father. It is good for the soul's health to begin the day by taking a satisfying draught from the river of the water of life. Very much more depends upon beginnings than some men think. How you go to bed tonight may be determined by your getting up this morning. If you get out of bed on the wrong side, you may keep on the wrong side all the day. If your heart be right in the waking, it will be a help toward its being right until sleeping. Go not forth into a dry world until the morning dew lies on your branch. Baptize your heart in devotion before you wade into the stream of daily care. See not the face of man until you have first seen the face of God. Let your first thoughts fly heavenward, and let your first breathings be prayer.

And now we are downstairs, and are off to business or to labor. As you hurry along the street, think of these words, "Be thou in the fear of the LORD all the day long." Leave not your God at home. You need Him most abroad. In mingling with your fellowmen, be with them, but be not *of* them, if that would involve your forgetting your Lord. That early interview which you have had with your Beloved should perfume your conversation all the day. A smile from Jesus in the morning will be sunshine all the day. Endeavor, when you are plying the trowel, or driving the plane, or guiding the plow, or using the needle or the pen, to keep up constant communication with your Father and your Lord. Let the telephone between you and the Eternal never cease from its use. Do put your ear to it and hear what the Lord shall speak to you. Do put your mouth to it and ask counsel from the oracle above. Whether you work long hours or short hours, "Be in the fear of the LORD all the day long."

But it is time for meals—be in the fear of the Lord at your table. The soul may be poisoned while the body is being nourished if we turn the hour of refreshment into an hour of indulgence. Some have been gluttonous, more have been drunken. Do not think of your table as though it were a hog's trough where the animal might gorge to the full. But watch your appetite, and by holy thanksgiving make your table to be the Lord's table. So eat the bread of earth as to eat bread at last in the kingdom of God. So drink that your head and heart may be in the best condition to serve God. When God feeds you do not profane the occasion by excess or defile it by loose conversation.

During the day our business calls us into company. Our associations in labor may not be so choice as we could wish; but he that earns his bread is often thrown where his own will would not lead him. If we were never to deal with ungodly men, it would be necessary for us to go out of the world. He that is in the fear of God all the day long will watch his own spirit and language and actions that these may be such as become the Gospel of Christ in whatever society his lot may be cast. Seek not to be a hermit or a monk, but be a man of God among men. When making a bargain or selling your goods to customers, be in the fear of God. It may be needful to go into the market or on the exchange, but be in the fear of the Lord amid the throng. It may be you will seldom be able to speak of that which is most dear to you, lest you cast pearls before swine. But you must abide always under holy and heavenly influence, so as to be always ready to give a reason for the hope which is in you with meekness and fear. "Be thou in the fear of the LORD all the day long," though your ears may be vexed and your heart grieved with the evil around you. He that cannot be in the fear of God in London cannot in the country.

The company have now gone, and you are alone. Maintain the fear of the Lord in your solitude. Beware of falling into solitary sin. Certain young men and women, when alone, pull out a wicked novel which they would not like to be seen reading. Others will have their sly nips though they would be reputed very temperate. If a man be right with God he is in his best company when alone. He seeks therein to honor his God and not to grieve Him. Surely, when I am alone with God, I am bound to use my best manners. Do nothing which you would be afraid to have known. Be in the fear of the Lord when you are so much alone that you have no fear of men.

The evening draws in, the shop is closed, and you have a little time to yourself. Our young people in shops need a rest and a walk. Is this your case? "Be thou in the fear of the LORD all the day long." In the evening, as well as in the morning, be true to your Lord. Beware of ill company in the evening! Take care that you never say, "Surely the darkness shall cover me." "Be thou in the fear of the LORD" when sinners entice you, and at once refuse any offer which is not pleasing to God.

"Recreation," says one. Yes, recreation. There are many helpful and healthy recreations which can in moderation be used to advantage. But engage in no pastime which would hinder your continuing in the fear of the Lord. In your recreation forget not your higher *recreation* wherein you were created anew in Christ Jesus. Our chief rest lies in a change of service for our Lord; our fullest pleasure is fellowship with Jesus.

Night has fallen around us, and we are home with our families. Let us not forget to close the day with family prayer and private prayer, as we opened it. Our chamber must see nothing which angels might blush to look upon. Those holy beings come and go where holy ones repose. Angels have a special liking for sleeping saints. Did they not put a ladder from heaven down to the place where Jacob lay? Though he had only a stone for his pillow, the earth for his bed, the hedges for his curtains, and the skies for his canopy, yet God was there, and angels flocked about him. Between God's throne and the beds of holy men there has long been a much frequented road. Sleep in Jesus every night so that you may sleep in Jesus at the last. From dawn to midnight "be thou in the fear of the LORD."

Let us now remember special occasions. All days are not quite the same. Exceptional events will happen, and these are all included in the day. You sustain, perhaps, one day a great loss, and unexpectedly find yourself far poorer than when you left your bed. "Be thou in the fear of the LORD" when under losses and adversities. When the great water-floods prevail and storms of trials sweep over you, remain in the ark of the fear of the Lord, and you shall be as safe as Noah was.

Possibly you may have a wonderful day of success, but be not always gaping for it. Yet your ship may come home; your windfall may drop at your feet. Beyond anything you have expected, a surprising gain may fall into your lap. Be not unduly excited, but remain in the fear of the Lord. Take heed that you be not lifted up with pride, so as to dote upon your wealth, for then your God may find it needful to afflict you out of love to your soul.

It may happen, during the day, that you are assailed by an unusual temptation. Christian men are well armed against common temptations, but sudden assaults may injure them. Therefore, "be in the fear of the LORD all the day long," and then surprises will not overthrow you. You shall not be afraid of evil tidings, neither shall you be betrayed by evil suggestions, if you be rooted and grounded in the constant fear of the Lord.

During the day, perhaps, you are maliciously provoked. An evil person assails you with envenomed speech. If you lose your temper even a little, your adversary takes advantage of your weakness, and becomes more bitter and slanderous. He hurls at you things which ought not to be thought of, much less to be said. "Be thou in the fear of the LORD all the day long"; "Cease from anger, and forsake wrath"; "Be not overcome of evil, but overcome evil with good." The adversary knows your tender place, and therefore he says the most atrocious things against God and holy things. Heed him not; but in patience possess your soul, and in the fear of the Lord you will find an armor which his poisoned arrows cannot pierce. "May the peace of God which passeth all understanding, keep your hearts and minds through Christ Jesus."

It may be that during the day you will have to act in a very difficult business. Common transactions between man and man are easy enough to honest minds. But every now and then a nice point is raised, a point of conscience, a matter not to be decided off-hand: "Be thou in the fear of the LORD all the day long." Spread the hard case before the Lord.

Judge a matter as it will be judged before His bar. If this be too much for your judgment, then wait upon God for further light. No man goes astray even in a difficult case if he is accustomed to cry like David, "Bring hither the ephod." This holy Book and the divine Spirit will guide us aright when our best judgment wavers. "Be thou in the fear of the LORD all the day long."

But, alas! you are feeling very unwell; this day will differ from those of activity. You cannot go to business; you have to keep to your bed. Fret not, but "be in the fear of the LORD all the day long." If the day has to last through the night because sleep forsakes you, be still with your thoughts soaring toward heaven, your desires quiet in your Father's bosom, and your mind happy in the sympathy of Christ. To have our whole being bathed and baptized in the Holy Spirit is to find health in sickness and joy in pain.

It may be, also, that you suffer from a mental sickness in the form of depression of spirit. Things look very dark and your heart is very heavy. Mourner, "Be thou in the fear of the LORD all the day long." When life is like a foggy day—when providence is cloudy and stormy and you are caught in a hurricane—still "be in the fear of the LORD." When your soul is exceeding sorrowful and you are bruised as a cluster trodden in the wine-press, yet cling close to God and never let go your reverent fear of Him. However exceptional and unusual may be your trial, yet vow within your soul, "Though he slay me, yet will I trust in him."

I have sketched the matter roughly. *Let me now suggest to you excellent reasons* for being always in the fear of the Lord. Ought we not to be in the fear of the Lord all the day long, since He sees us all the day long? Does the Lord ever take His eye from off us? Does the keeper of Israel ever slumber? If God were not our God but only our lawful master, I should say, "Let us not be eye-servants." But since we cannot escape His all-seeing eye, let us be the more careful how we behave ourselves. "Be thou in the fear of the LORD all the day long," for Jehovah, whom thou fearest, sees you without ceasing.

Remember, also, that sin is equally evil all the day long. Is there an hour when it would be right to disobey God? Is there some interval in which the law of holiness has no force? I know not. Therefore, never consent to sin. To fear God is always right. To put away the fear of God from before our eyes would be always criminal, therefore, be ever in the fear of God. Remember the strictness of Nehemiah's integrity and how he said, "So did not I because of the fear of the Lord."

Walk in the fear of the Lord at all times because you always belong to Christ. The blood-mark is always upon you. Will you ever belie it? You have been chosen, and you are always chosen. You have been bought with a price, and you are always your Lord's. You have been called out from the world by the Holy Spirit, and He is always calling you. You have been preserved by sovereign grace, and you are always so preserved. Therefore, by the privileges you enjoy, you are bound to abide in the fear of the Lord. How could you lay down your God-given and heaven-honored character of a child of God? No, rather cling forever to your adoption and the heritage it secures you.

You can never tell when Satan will attack you, therefore be always in the fear of the Lord. You are in an enemy's country. Soldiers, be always on the watch! Soldiers, keep in order of fight! You might straggle from the ranks and begin to lie about in the hedges and sleep without sentries if you were in your own country. But you are marching through the foeman's land, where an enemy lurks behind every bush. The fear of the Lord is your sword and shield; never lay it down.

Furthermore, remember that your Lord may come at any hour. Before the word can travel from my lip to your ear Jesus may be here. While you are in business or on your bed or in the field, the flaming heavens may proclaim His advent. Stand, therefore, with your loins girt and your lamps trimmed ready to go into the supper whenever the Bridegroom comes, or you may die. As a church we have had a double warning during the last few days in the departure of our two beloved elders, Messrs. Hellier and Croker. They have been carried home like shocks of corn, fully ripe. They have departed in peace and have joyfully entered into rest. We also are on the margin of the dividing stream. Our feet are dipped in the waters which wash the river's brim. We, too, shall soon ford the black torrent. In a moment, suddenly, we may be called away. Let every action be such that we would not object to have it quoted as our last action. Let every day be so spent that it might fitly be the close of life on earth. Let our near and approaching end help to keep us "in the fear of the LORD all the day long."

If we keep in that state, *observe the admirable results!* To abide in the fear of the Lord is to dwell safely. To forsake the Lord would be to court danger. In the fear of the Lord there is strong confidence, but apart from it there is no security. How honorable is such a state! Men ridicule the religion which is not uniform. I heard of a brother who claimed to have long been a teetotaler, but some doubted. When he was asked how long he had been an abstainer, he replied, "Off and on, for twenty years." You should have seen the significant smile upon all faces. An abstainer off and on! His example did not stand for much. Certain professors are Christians "off and on," and nobody respects them. Such seed as this will not grow. There is no vitality in it. Constancy is the proof of sincerity. "Be thou in the fear of the LORD all the day long"—this is to be happy. God has spoiled the believer for being easy in sin. If you are a Christian you will never find happiness in departing from God. I say again, God has spoiled you for such pleasure. Your joy lies in a closer walk with God. Your heaven on earth is in communion with the Lord.

If you abide in the fear of the Lord, how useful you will be! Your "off and on" people are worth nothing. Nobody is influenced by them. What little good they do, they undo. The abiding man is also the growing man. He that is "in the fear of the LORD all the day long" gets to have more of that fear. It has more practical power over his life and heart. What a poor life they lead who are alternately zealous and lukewarm! Like Penelope, they weave by day, but unravel by night. They blow hot and cold, and so melt and freeze by turns. They build and then break down, and so are never at rest. Children of God, let your conduct be consistent. Let not your lives be like a draught-board with as many blacks as whites. Do not be speckled birds—like magpies, more famed for chatter than anything else. Oh, that God would make us white doves! I pray you be not bold one day and cowardly another. Be not one day sound in the faith, and the next day on the downgrade. Be not under excitement generous, and in cool blood mean as a miser. Oh, that we might become like our Father in heaven in holiness, and then become like Him in immutability, so as to be forever holy!

From all this *let us infer our great need*. I think I hear somebody say, "You are cutting out a nice bit of work for us." Am I? Believe me, I am looking to a stronger hand than yours. To be in the fear of the Lord for a single day is not to be accomplished by unrenewed nature; it is a work of grace. See, then, what great grace you will need for all the days of your life. Go for it, and get it. See how little you can do without the Spirit of God. Without His indwelling you will soon cast off all fear of the Lord. Plead the covenant promise, "I will put my fear in their hearts, that they shall not depart from me." Depend upon God for everything. As you know that salvation is of faith that it might be by grace, exercise much faith toward God. Believe that He can make you to be in His fear all the day long. "According to your faith, be it unto you." Believe holiness to be possible; seek after it, and possess it. Faith, as it is the channel of grace, must always be associated with truth. True faith lives on truth. If you give up the doctrines of the Gospel, you will not be in the fear of God at all. If you begin to doubt them, you will not be "in the fear of the LORD all the day long." Get solid truth for the foundation of your faith, and let your firm faith bring you daily grace that you may manifestly be always in the fear of the Lord.

The Probable Interruption

It has happened to godly men in all ages to see *the wicked prosper,* and they have been staggered by the sight. You see a man who has no conscience making money in your trade, while you make none.

Sometimes you think that your conscientiousness hinders you. I hope it is nothing else. You see another person scheming and cheating. To him honesty is mere policy, and Sabbath labor is no difficulty, for the Word of God is nothing to him. You cannot do as he does, and therefore you do not seem to get on as he does. Be it so, but let not his prosperity grieve you. There is something better to live for than mere money-making. If your life pleases God, let it please you. Never envy the ungodly. Suppose God allows them to succeed—what then? You should no more envy them than you envy fat bullocks the ribbons which adorn them at the show. They are ready for the slaughter. Do you wish yourself in their place? The fate of the prosperous sinner is one to be dreaded. He is set on high to be cast down.

Do not even in your wish deprive the ungodly of their transient happiness. Their present prosperity is the only heaven they will ever know. Let them have as much of it as they can. I have heard of a wife who treated her unkind and ungodly husband with great gentleness for this very reason. She said, "I have prayed for him and entreated him to think about his soul. But at last I have come to fear that he will die in his sins. Therefore I have made up my mind that I will make him as happy as I can in this life. I tremble to think of what his misery must be in the world to come, and therefore I will make him happy *now*." O men in your senses, surely you will not grudge poor swine their husks and swill! No, fill the trough and let the creature feed, for it has neither part nor lot in a higher life. Believer, take your bitter cup and drink it without complaining, for an hour with your God will be a hundredfold recompense for a life of trial.

One is the more tried because *these men are very apt to boast*. They crow over the suffering believer saying, "What comes of your religion? You are worse off than I am. See how splendidly I get on without God!" Care nothing for their boasting. It will end so soon. Their tongue walks through the earth, but it only utters vanity.

It is galling to see *the enemies of God triumphant*. Their policy for a time beats the plain protest of the lover of truth. Their deceit baffles the plain man. The lovers of error outnumber the men of God. Such men tread on creeds and trust-deeds and every other legal protection of honest people. What care they? They despise the old-fashioned folk whom they oppress. Remember Haman in the Book of Esther, and note how glorious he was until he was hung up on the gallows.

There is no real cause for envying the wicked; for their present is danger, their future is doom. I see them now on yonder island, sporting, dancing, feasting merrily. I am standing as on a bare rock, and I might well envy them their island of roses and lilies. But as I watch I see that their fairy island is gradually sinking to destruction. The ocean is rising all around; the waves are carrying away the shores. Even while they dance the floods advance. Lo, yonder is one infatuated wretch sinking amidst the devouring flood. The rest continue at their play, but it cannot last much longer. They will soon be gone. Let me stand on my lone rock, rather than sink amid their fleeting luxury. Let me abide in safety rather than dance where danger is all around.

Aye, dear friends, if you envy the wicked *it will do you serious harm*. Envy helps in no way, but it hinders in many ways. If you envy the wicked you may soon wish to be like them. If you do so wish, you are like them now! He that would be willing to be wicked in order to prosper is wicked already. He who says, "I should like to do as they do that I might grow rich as they do," why, he is a man that has his price and would sell his soul if he could meet a purchaser. No, not for all the world would we share the lot of unbelievers. We would sit in the gate with Mordecai sooner than feast with the king with Haman. God help us, dear friends, that we may not be disturbed by seeing the prosperity of the wicked.

The Helpful Consideration

The text says, "For surely there is an end; and thine expectation shall not be cut off." First, then, *there is an end of this life*. These things are not forever. On the contrary, all that we see is a dissolving view. Surely, every man walks in a vain show; even as a show it is vain. You talk of spiritual things as though they were shadows; but in very truth these are the only substance. Temporal things are as the mirage of the desert. The things about us are such stuff as dreams are made of. When we truly awake we shall despise their image. In all wealth and honor there are a worm and a moth. Think of the sinner's end, and you will no longer be troubled when he spreads himself like a green bay tree.

Next, *there is an end of the worldling's prosperity*. He makes his money. What then? He makes more. What then? He makes more. What then? He dies. And then there is a little notice in the newspaper which says that he died worth so much; which, being interpreted, means that he was taken away from so much that he never possessed, but guarded for his heir. There is an end in death, and after death the judgment— "for God shall bring every work into judgment, with every secret thing." What an end will that be! The sinner may live as carelessly as he pleases, but he must answer for it at the judgment seat of Christ. Loud may be his laughter, sarcastic and bitter may be his criticisms upon religion. But there is an end and when the death-sweat beads his brow, he will lower his key and need help from that very Gospel which he criticized. "There is an end." Let us not spend our lives for that which has an end. An immortal soul should seek immortal joys.

Dear friends, to you there is an end in quite another sense. *God has an end in your present trouble and exercise.* Your difficulties and trials are sent as messengers from God with gracious design. "Be thou in the fear of the LORD all the day long," for every part of the day has its tendency to work out your spiritual education, your preparation for the heaven to come. In everything that happens to you your heavenly Father has an end. The arrows of calamity are aimed at your sins. Your bitter cups are meant to purify the inward parts of the soul. Fret not, but trust. There is an old proverb that you should never let children and fools see half-finished works. Even so, the work of God in providence cannot be judged of by such poor children as we are, for we cannot see to the end of the Lord's design. My friends, when we see the end from the beginning and behold God's work complete, we shall have a very different view of things from what we have now while the work is still proceeding.

Lastly, while there is an end to the wicked, *there will be no failure to your expectation.* What are you expecting? That God will keep His promise? And so He will. That God will give you peace in the end? And so He will. That He will raise you from the dead and set you in heavenly places with Christ? And so He will. And that you shall be forever with the Lord, and He will grant you glory and bliss? And so He will. "Your expectation shall not be cut off." Every Christian is a man of great expectations, and none of them will fail. Let him cultivate his hope and enlarge its scope, for the hopes which are built on Jesus and His grace will never disappoint us. In our case the birds in the bush are better birds than those in the hand, and they are quite as sure. The promise of God is in itself a possession, and our expectation of it is in itself an enjoyment.

I have done, dear friends. May the Holy Spirit speak these things home to your hearts! Christian people ought to be exceedingly glad. If they have but a small estate, they have it on an endless tenure. The worldling may have a large house, but he has it only upon a short lease. He will have nothing soon. Just now there is a great noise made about leaseholds falling in. Every ungodly man may have his life-lease run out tomorrow! But the believer has a freehold. What he has is his without reserve. "Their inheritance shall be for ever." By faith grasp the eternal. Treasure the spiritual. Rejoice in God, and "be in the fear of the LORD all the day long." God grant you this in His great grace, for Christ's sake! Amen.

10

Tomorrow

Boast not thyself of tomorrow; for thou knowest not what a day may bring forth (Proverbs 27:1).

God's most Holy Word was principally written to inform us of the way to heaven, and to guide us in our path through this world to the realms of eternal life and light. But as if to teach us that God is not careless concerning our doings in the present scene and that our benevolent Father is not inattentive to our happiness, even in this state, He has furnished us with some excellent and wise maxims, which we may put in practice, not only in spiritual matters, but in temporal affairs also. I have always looked upon the book of Proverbs with pleasure as being a book not only teaching us the highest spiritual wisdom, but as also more especially speaking on the "now"—the time that is present with us—giving us maxims that will make us wise for this world and that will instruct us in conducting our affairs while we are here among our fellowmen. We need some temporal wisdom as well as spiritual illumination.

It need not always be that the children of the kingdom should be more foolish than the children of darkness. It is well that we should be wise to order our common affairs aright, as well as to set our house in order for the grave. Hence we find in Scripture maxims and teachings for them both. Since God has been pleased thus to instruct us in the avocations of life, I shall not, then, be out of place if I use my text, in some degree, in a merely temporal manner, and endeavor to give advice to my friends concerning the business of this life. Afterward, I shall dwell upon it more spiritually. There is, first, *the abuse of tomorrow* forbidden in the text. In the second place, I shall mention *the right use of tomorrow.*

This sermon was taken from *The New Park Street Pulpit* and was preached on Monday afternoon, August 25, 1856.

The Abuse of Tomorrow

We shall look upon it first in a worldly point of view, and yet, I trust, in a way of wisdom. "Boast not thyself of tomorrow." Oh! my friends, whosoever you be, whether you be Christians or no, this passage has a depth of wisdom in it for you. "Boast not thyself of tomorrow," and this, for many very wise reasons.

First of all, *because it is extremely foolish to boast at all.* Boasting never makes a man any the greater in the esteem of others, nor does it improve the real estate either of his body or soul. Let a man brag as he will, he is none the greater for his bragging. No, he is the less, for men invariably think the worse of him. Let him boast as much as he pleases of anything that he possesses, he shall not increase its value by his glorying. He cannot multiply his wealth by boasting of it; he cannot increase his pleasures by glorying in them. True, to be content with those pleasures and feel a complacency in them may render them very sweet. But not so with such a treasure as this, for it is a treasure which he has not yet, and, therefore, how foolish he is to glory in it. There is an old, old proverb, which I dare not quote here. It is something to do with chickens. Perhaps you can recollect it. It bears very well upon this text, for tomorrow is a thing that we have not yet obtained. Therefore, not only if we had it would it be foolish to boast of it, but because we have it not, and may never have it, it becomes the very extremity of foolishness to glory in it.

Glory, O man, in the harvest that may come to you next year when your seed is sown. But glory not in tomorrow, for you can sow no seeds of morrows. Morrows come from God; you have no right to glory in them. Glory if you will, O fowler, that the birds have once flown to your net, for they may come again. But glory not too soon, for they may find another decoy that shall be better to their taste than yours, or they may rove far off from your snare. Though many a day has come to you, think not that another will certainly arrive. Days are not like links of a chain; one does not ensure the other. We have one, but we may never see its fellow; each may be the last of its kind. Each springs of a separate birth. There are no twin days. Today has no brother, it stands alone, and tomorrow must come alone, and the next and the next, also, must be born into this world without a brother. We must never look upon two days at once, nor expect that a whole herd of days shall be brought forth at one time

We need not boast of tomorrow, for *it is one of the frailest things in all creation,* and therefore, the least to be boasted of. Boast of the bubbles on the breaker, boast of the foam upon the sea, boast of the clouds that skim the sky, boast of what you will, O man, but boast not of tomorrow, for it is too unsubstantial. Tomorrow, it is a fleeting thing. You have not seen it. Why do you boast of it? Tomorrow, it is the cup which the idiot dreams lies at the foot of the rainbow. It is not there, nor has he found it. Tomorrow—it is the floating island of Loch Lomond—many have talked of it, but none have seen it. Tomorrow—it is the wrecker's beacon, enticing men to the rock of destruction. Boast not yourself of tomorrow. It is the frailest and most brittle thing you can imagine. Not glass were half so easily broken as your tomorrow's joys and your tomorrow's hopes. A puff of wind shall crush them, while yet they seem not to be full blown. He said, good easy man, full surely my greatness is a ripening, but there came a frost—a killing frost—which nipped his shoot and then he fell. Boast not of tomorrow; you have it not. Boast not of tomorrow; you may never have it. Boast not of tomorrow; if you had it, it would deceive you. Boast not of tomorrow, for tomorrow you may be where morrows will be dreadful things to tremble at.

Boast not yourself of tomorrow, not only because it is extremely foolish, but *because it is exceedingly hurtful.* Boasting of tomorrow is hurtful to us every way. It is hurtful to us now. I never knew a man who was always hoping to do great things in the future that ever did much in the present. I never knew a man who intended to make a fortune by-and-by who ever saved sixpence a week now. I never knew a man who had very great and grand hopes on the death of some old grandmother, or the coming-in of some property from chancery, or the falling to him of something because his name was Jenyns. I never saw him very prosperous in the meantime. I have heard of a man going to be rich tomorrow and boasting of it, but I never knew him do much. Such men spend so much time in building castles in the air that they have no stones left wherewith to build so much as a cottage on the ground. They were wasting all their energies on tomorrow. Consequently they had no time to reap the fields of the present, for they were waiting for the heavy harvests of the future. The heavily laden boats of today come in with abundance of fish from the depths of time. But they said of them, "They are nothing. There will be heavier draughts tomorrow. There will be greater abundance then. Go away, little ships; an aritosy shall come home tomorrow—a very fleet of wealth." So they let today's wealth go by because they expected the greater wealth of tomorrow. Therefore, they were hurt even for the present.

And worse than that, *some men were led into extraordinary extravagance* from their hopes of the future. They spend what they are going to have, or rather what they never will have. Many have been ruined by the idle dream of speculation. What is that but boasting of tomorrow? They have said, "True, I cannot pay for this which I now purchase. But

I shall tomorrow, for tomorrow I shall roll in wealth. Tomorrow, perhaps, I shall be the richest of men. A lucky turn of business (as they term it) will lift me off this shoal." So they keep still, and not only do they refuse to toil to push themselves off the sand, but worse than that, they are throwing themselves away and wasting what they have in the hope of better times coming in the future. Many a man has been made halt, lame, blind, and dumb in the present because he hoped to be greater than a man in the future.

I always laugh at those who say to me, "Sir, rest a while. You will work all the longer for it. Stay a while, lest you waste your strength, for you may work tomorrow." I bid them remember that such is not the teaching of Scripture, for that says, "Whatsoever thy hand findeth to do, do it with thy might." I would count myself worse than a fool if I should throw away my todays in the expectation of tomorrows, and rest upon the couch of idleness today, because I thought the chariot of tomorrow would make up for all my sloth. No, beloved, if we love our God, we shall find enough to do, if we have all our tomorrows and use all our todays too. If we serve our God as we ought to serve Him, considering what He has done for us, we shall find that we shall have more than our hands full, let our life be spared as long as Methuselah's—enough for every moment, enough for every hour, long as life may be. But hoping to do things in the future takes away our strength in the present, unnerves our resolution, and unstrings our diligence. Let us take care that we are not hurt in the present by boasting of tomorrow.

And, remember, that if you boast of tomorrow, it will not only hurt you today, but *hurt you tomorrow also*. Do you know why? Because, as sure as you are alive, you will be disappointed with tomorrow if you boast of it before it comes. Tomorrows would be very good things if you did not give them such a very good character. I believe one of the very worst things a minister can possess is to have anybody to recommend him. For the people say, "Here comes a man, how he will preach, how eloquent he will be!" The poor creature cannot come up to their expectations, and so they are disappointed. So with tomorrow, you give him such flattering encomiums. "Oh! he is everything; he is perfection." Todays—they are nothing. They are the very sweepings of the floors. But tomorrows—they are the solid gold. Todays—they are exhausted mines, and we get little from them. But tomorrows—they are the very mines of wealth. We have only to get them, and we are rich, immensely rich. The tomorrows are everything. Then the tomorrows come laden with mercy and big with blessings of God. But, notwithstanding, we are disappointed because tomorrow is not what we expected it to be, even when tomorrow is marvelously abundant. But sometimes tomorrow comes with storms, and clouds, and darkness when we expected it to be full of light and sunshine. Oh, how terrible is our feeling then from the very reason that we expected something different. It is not at all a bad beatitude, "Blessed is the man that expecteth nothing, for he shall never be disappointed."

If we know how to practice that and expect nothing, we shall not be disappointed, it is certain. The less we expect and the less we boast of our expectations, the more happy will the future be because we shall have far less likelihood of being disappointed. Let us recollect, then, that if we would kill the future, if we would ruin the tomorrows, if we would blast their hopes, if we would take away their honey, we must press them in the hand of boasting, and then we shall have done it. "Boast not thyself of tomorrow," for you spoil the tomorrow by boasting of it.

And then, remember, *what solemnly disastrous circumstances have occurred to men in this life* after tomorrow had gone from boasting of tomorrows. Aye, there is many a man that set all his hope upon one single thing. The tomorrow came which he did not expect—perhaps a black and dark tomorrow—and it crushed his hopes to ashes. How sad he felt afterward! He was in his nest. He said, "Peace, peace, peace," and sudden destruction came upon his happiness and his joy. He had boasted of his tomorrow by over security. See him there, what a very wreck of a man he is because he had set his hope on that. Now his joy is blasted. Oh! my friends, never boast too much of the tomorrows because if you do, your disappointment will be tremendous when you shall find your joys have failed you and your hopes have passed away. See there that rich man. He has piled heaps on heaps of gold. But now for a desperate venture, he is about to have more than he ever possessed before and reckons on that tomorrow. Nothingness is his. What is his disappointment? Because he boasted of imagined wealth. See that man! His ambition is to raise his house and perpetuate his name. See that heir of his—his joy, his life, his fullness of happiness. A handful of ashes and a coffin are left to the weeping father. Oh! if he had not boasted too much of the certainty of that son's life, he had not wept so bitterly after the tomorrow had swept over him with all its blast and mildew of his expectations. See yonder, another, he is famous; he is great. Tomorrow comes a slander, and his fame is gone and his name disgraced. Oh! had he not set his love on that, he had not cared whether men cried, "crucify," or "hallelujah." He had disregarded both alike. But believing that fame was a stable thing, whereas its foot is on the sand, he reckoned on tomorrows. Mark how sad he walks the earth because tomorrow has brought him nothing but grief. "Boast not thyself of tomorrow."

And I would have you remember just one fact—and that I think to be a very important one—that very often when men boast of tomorrow, and are overconfident that they shall live, *they not only entail great sorrow upon themselves, but upon others also*. I have, when preaching, frequently begged of my friends to be quite sure to make their wills and see to their family affairs. Many are the solemn instances which should urge you to do so. One night a minister happened to say in the course of his sermon that he held it to be a Christian duty for every man to have his house set in order, so that if he were taken away, he would know, that as far as possible, everything would be right. And there was one member of his church there who said to himself, "What my minister has said is true. I should not like to see my babes and my wife left with nothing, as they must be if I were to die." So he went home. That night he made his will and cleared up his accounts. That night he died! It must have been a joyful thing for the widow, in the midst of her sadness, to find herself amply provided for and everything in order for her comfort. Good Whitfield said he could not lie down in bed at night if he did not know that even his gloves were in their place. He said he should not like to die with anything in his house out of order. And I would have every Christian very careful, to be so living one day, that if he were never to see another, he might feel that he had done the utmost that he could, not only to provide for himself, but also for those who inherit his name and are dear to him. Perhaps you call this only worldly teaching—very good. You will find it very much like heavenly teaching one of these dark days, if you do not practice it. "Boast not thyself of tomorrow."

The Spiritual Manner of Tomorrow

But now I come to dwell upon this in *a spiritual manner* for a moment or two. "Boast not thyself of tomorrow." Oh! my beloved friends, never boast of tomorrow with regard to your soul's salvation.

They do so in the first place *who think that it will be easier for them to repent tomorrow than it is today*. Felix said there would be a more convenient season, and then he would again send for Paul that he might hear him seriously. And many a sinner thinks that just now it is not easy to turn and to repent, but that by-and-by it will be. Now, is not that a very string of falsehoods? In the first place, is it ever easy for a sinner to turn to God? Must not that be done, at any time, by divine power? And again, if that be not easy for him *now,* how will it be easier in after life? Will not his sins bind fresh fetters to his soul, so that it will be even more impossible for him to escape from his iron bondage? If he be dead now, will he not be corrupt before he reaches tomorrow? And when tomorrow comes, to which he looks forward as being easier for a resurrection, will not his soul be yet more corrupt, and therefore, if we may so speak, even further from the possibility of being raised? Oh!

sirs, you say it is easy for you to repent tomorrow. Why, then, not today? You would find the difficulty of it, if you should try it. Yes, you would find your own helplessness in that matter. Possibly you dream that on a future day repentance will be more agreeable to your feelings. But how can you suppose that a few hours will make it more pleasant? If it be vinegar to your taste now, it shall be so then. If you love your sins now, you will love them better then, for the force of habit will have confirmed you in your course. Every moment of your lives is driving in another rivet to your eternal state. So far as we can see, it becomes less and less likely (speaking after the manner of men) that the sinner should burst his chains each sin that he commits, for habit has bound him yet faster to his guilt, and his iniquity has gotten another hold upon him. Let us take care, then, that we do not boast of tomorrow by a pretense that it will be so much easier to repent tomorrow. Whereas, it is one of Satan's lies, for it will only be the more difficult.

He boasts of tomorrow, again, *who supposes that he shall have plenty of time to repent and to return to God*. Oh! there are many who say, "When I come to die, I shall be on my deathbed, and then I shall say, 'Lord, have mercy upon me a sinner.'" I remember an aged minister telling me a story of a man whom he often warned, but who always said to him, "Sir, when I am dying, I shall say 'Lord, have mercy on me.' And I shall go to heaven as well as anybody else." Returning home from market one night, rather "fou" with liquor, he guided his horse with a leap right over the parapet of a bridge into the river. The last words he was heard to utter were a most fearful imprecation. In the bed of the river he was found dead, killed by the fall. So it may be with you. You think you will have space for repentance, and it may be that sudden doom will devour you. Or, perhaps, even while you are sitting there in the pew, your last moment is running out. There is your hour-glass. See! it is running. I marked another grain just then, and then another fell. It fell so noiselessly, yet I thought I heard it fall. Yes! there it is! The clock's tick is the fall of that grain of dust down from your hour-glass. Life is getting shorter every moment with all of you. But with some the sand is almost out, there is not a handful left. A few more grains. See, now they are less, two or three. Oh! in a moment it may be said, "There is not one left." Sinner! never think that you have time to spare! You never had; man never had.

God says, "Haste thee," when He bids men flee from Sodom. Lot had to haste. Depend upon it, when the Spirit speaks in a man's heart, he does always bid him haste. Under natural convictions, men are very prone to tarry. But the Spirit of God, when He speaks in the heart of man, always says, "today." I never knew a truly anxious soul, yet, who was willing to put off until tomorrow. When God the Holy Spirit has dealings with a man, they are always immediate dealings. The sinner is impatient to get deliverance. He must have pardon now. He must have present mercy, or else he fears that mercy will come too late to him. Let me beseech you, then (and may God the Holy Spirit grant that my entreaty may become successful in your case), that there is never time to spare. That your thought that there is time to spare is an insinuation of Satan, for when the Spirit pleads with man, He pleads with him with demands of immediate attention. "*Today,* if you will hear his voice, harden not your hearts, as in the provocation."

"Boast not thyself of tomorrow," O sinner, as I doubt not you are doing in another fashion. "Boast not thyself of tomorrow," *in the shape of resolves to do better.* I think I have given up resolutions now. I have enough of the *debris* and the rubbish of my resolutions to build a cathedral with if they could but be turned into stone. Oh! the broken resolutions, the broken vows, all of us have had! Oh! we have raised castles of resolution, structures of enormous size, that outvied Babylon itself in all its majesty. Says one, "I know I shall be better tomorrow. I shall renounce this vice and the other. I shall forsake this lust. I shall give up that darling sin. True, I shall not do so now—a little more sleep and a little more slumber—but I know I shall do it tomorrow." Fool! you know not that you shall see tomorrow. Oh! greater fool! You ought to know that what you are not willing to do today, you will not be willing to do tomorrow. I believe there are many souls that have been lost by good intentions which were never carried out. Resolutions strangled at their birth brought on men the guilt of spiritual infanticide. They have been lost with resolutions sticking in their mouths. Many a man has gone down to hell with a good resolution on his lips, with a pious resolve on his tongue. Oh! if he had lived another day, he said he would have been so much better. If he lied lived another week, oh, then he thought he would begin to pray. Poor soul! if he had been spared another week, he would only have sunk deeper into sin! But he did not think so, and he went to hell with a choice morsel rolling under his tongue—that he should do better directly and that he meant to amend by-and-by.

There are many of you present, I dare say, who are making good resolutions. You are apprentices. Well, you are not going to carry them out until you get to be journeymen. You are journeymen. Well, you cannot carry them out until you get to be master. You have been breaking the Sabbath, but you intend to leave it off when you are in another situation. You have been accustomed to swear. You say, "I shall not swear any more when I get out of this company, they try my temper so." You have committed this or that petty theft. Tomorrow you will renounce it, because tomorrow you will have enough, and you can afford to do it. But of all the lying things—and there are many things that are deceptive—resolutions for tomorrow are the worst of all. I would not trust one of them. There is nothing stable in them. You might sooner sail to America across the Atlantic on a sere leaf than float to heaven on a resolution.

It is the frailest thing in the world, tossed about by every circumstance, and wrecked with all its precious freight—wrecked to the dismay of the man who ventured his soul in it—wrecked, and wrecked for aye. Take care, my dear hearers, that none of you are reckoning on tomorrows. I remember the strong but solemn words of Jonathan Edwards, where he says, "Sinner, remember, thou art at this moment standing over the mouth of hell upon a single plank, and that plank is rotten; thou art hanging over the jaws of perdition by a solitary rope, and lo! the strands of that rope are creaking—breaking now, and yet thou talkest of to-morrows!" If you were sick, man, would you send for your physician tomorrow? If your house were on fire, would thou call "fire" tomorrow? If you were robbed in the street on your road home, would you cry "stop thief" tomorrow? No, surely; but you are wiser than that in natural concerns. But man is foolish, oh! too foolish in the things that concern his soul. Unless divine and infinite love shall teach him to number his days that he may apply his heart to true wisdom, he will still go on boasting of tomorrows until his soul has been destroyed by them.

Just one hint to the child of God. Ah! my beloved brother or sister, do not, I beseech you, boast of tomorrow yourself. David did it once. He said, "My mountain standeth firm, I shall never be moved." Do not boast of your tomorrows. You have feathered your nest pretty well. Aye, but you may have a thorn in it before the sun has gone down, and you will be glad enough to fly aloft. You are very happy and joyful, but do not say you will always have as much faith as you have now—do not be sure you will always be as blessed. The next cloud that sweeps the skies may drive many of your joys away. Do not say you have been kept hitherto, and you are quite sure you will be preserved from sin tomorrow. Take care of tomorrows. Many Christians go tumbling on without a bit of thought. Then, on a sudden, they tumble down and make a mighty mess of their profession. If they would only look sharp after the tomorrows—if they would only watch their paths instead of stargazing and boasting about them—their feet would be a great deal surer. True, God's child need not think of tomorrow as regards his soul's eternal security, for that is in the hand of Christ and safe forever. But as far as his profession and comfort and happiness are concerned, it will well become him to take care of his feet every day.

Do not get boasting. If you get boasting of tomorrow, you know the Lord's rule is always to send a canker where we put our pride. And so if you boast of tomorrow, you will have a moth in it before long. As sure as ever we glory in our wealth, it becomes cankered or it takes to itself wings and flies away. As certainly as we boast of tomorrow, the worm will gnaw its root as it did Jonah's gourd, and the tomorrow under which we rested shall, with drooping leaves, only stand a monument of our disappointment. Let us take care, Christian friends, that we do not waste the present time with hopes of tomorrow that we do not get proud, and so off our guard, by boasting of what we most assuredly shall be then, as we imagine.

The Right Use of Tomorrow

And now, in the last place, if tomorrows are not to be boasted of, are they good for nothing? No, blessed be God! There are a great many things we may do with tomorrows. We may not boast of them, but I will tell you what we may do with them if we are the children of God. We may always look forward to them with *patience and confidence* that they will work together for our good. We may say of the tomorrows, "I do not boast of them, but I am not frightened at them. I would not glory in them, but I will not tremble about them."

> What may be my future lot,
> Well I know concerns me not;
> This doth set my heart at rest,
> What my God appoints is best.

We may be very easy and very comfortable about tomorrow. We may remember that all our times are in His hands, that all events are at His command. Though we know not all the windings of the path of providence, yet *He* knows them all. They are all settled in His book, and our times are all ordered by His wisdom—whether they be

> Times of trial and of grief;
> Times of triumph and relief;
> Times the tempter's power to prove,
> Times to taste a Saviour's love:
> All must come, and last, and end,
> As shall please my heavenly Friend.

And, therefore, we may look upon the tomorrows as we see them in the rough bullion of time about to be minted into every day's expenditure. We may say of them all, "They shall all be gold. They shall all be stamped with the King's impress, and, therefore, let them come. They will not make me worse—they will work together for my good."

Yes, more, a Christian may rightly look forward to his tomorrows, not simply with resignation, but also with *joy*. Tomorrow to a Christian is a happy thing, it is one stage nearer glory. Tomorrow! It is one step nearer heaven to a believer. It is just one knot more that he has sailed across the dangerous sea of life, and he is so much the nearer to his eternal port—his blissful heaven. Tomorrow, it is a fresh lamp of fulfilled promise that God has placed in His firmament that the Christian may hail it as a guiding star in the future or at least as a light to cheer his path. Tomorrow, the Christian may rejoice at it. He may say of today, "O day, you may be black, but I shall bid you good-bye. For lo, I see tomorrow coming, and I shall mount upon its wings, and shall flee away and leave you and your sorrows far behind me."

And, moreover, the Christian may await tomorrow with even more than simple hope and joy. He may look forward to it with *ecstasy* in some measure, for he does not know but that tomorrow his Lord may come. Tomorrow Christ may be upon this earth, "for in such an hour as ye think not the Son of Man cometh." Tomorrow, all the glories of millennial splendor may be revealed. Tomorrow, the thrones of judgment may be set, and the fringe may summon the people to judgment. Tomorrow, we may be in heaven. Tomorrow, we may be on the breast of Christ. Tomorrow, aye, before then, this head may wear a crown, this hand may wave the palm, this lip may sing the song, this foot may tread the streets of gold, this heart may be full of bliss, immortal, everlasting, eternal. Be of good cheer, oh, fellow-Christian, tomorrow can have nothing black in it for you, for it must work for your good, but it may have in it a precious, precious jewel. It is an earthen pitcher, and it may have in it some dark black waters, but their bitterness is taken away by the cross. But perhaps, also, it may have in it the precious jewel of eternity, for wrapped up within tomorrow may be all the glories of immortality. Anoint your head with fresh oil of gladness at the prospect of each coming day. Boast not of tomorrow, but often comfort yourself with it. You have a right to do so. It cannot be a bad tomorrow to you. It may be the best day of your life, for it may be your last.

And yet, another hint. Tomorrow ought to be observed by Christians in the way of providence. Though we may not boast of tomorrow, yet we may seek to provide for tomorrow. On one occasion I pleaded for a benefit society, and not knowing a more appropriate text, I selected this, "Take no thought for the morrow, for tomorrow shall take thought for the things of itself." Some of my hearers, when I announced my text, feared the principle of it was altogether hostile to anything like an insurance or providing for the future, but I just showed them that it was not, as I looked upon it. It is a positive command that we are to take no anxious thought concerning tomorrow. Now, how can I do that? How can I put myself into such a position that I can carry out this commandment of taking no thought for tomorrow! If I were a man struggling in life, and had it in my power to insure for something which would take care of wife and family in after days, if I did not do it, you might preach to me to all eternity about not taking thought for tomorrow. But I could not help doing it, when I saw those I loved around me unprovided for. Let it be in God's Word, I could not practice it. I would still be at some time or other taking thought for tomorrow. But let me go to one of the many of the excellent institutions which exist, and let me see that all is provided for, I come home and say, "Now, I know how to practice Christ's command of taking no thought for the morrow. I pay the policy-money once a year, and I take no further thought about it, for I have no occasion to do so now, and have obeyed the very spirit and letter of Christ's command." Our Lord meant that we were to get rid of cares. Now it is apparent that those distressing cares are removed, and we are able to live above anxiety by that single process.

Now, if that is so, if there is anything that enables us to carry out Christ's commands, is it not in the very bowels of the commandments to do that? If God has pleased to put into the hearts of wise men to devise something that should in some way ameliorate the misfortunes of their kind, and relieve them from the distresses and casualties of God's providence, how can it but be our duty to avail ourselves of that wisdom which, doubtless, God gave to men, that we might thereby in these times be enabled to carry out in the fullest extent the meaning of that passage, "Take no thought for the morrow." Why, if a man says, "I shall take no thought for tomorrow, I will just spend all I get, and not think of doing anything or taking any thought for tomorrow," how is he going to pay his rent? Why, the text could not be carried out, if it meant what some people think. It cannot mean that we should carelessly live by the day, or else a man would spend all his money on Monday and have nothing left for the rest of the week. But that would be simple folly. It means that we should have no anxious, distressing thought about it. I am preaching about benefit societies. I would not attempt to recommend many of them. And I do not believe in the principles of half of them. I believe a great deal of mischief is done by their gatherings in alehouses and pothouses. But wherever there is a Christian society, I must endeavor to promote its welfare, for I look on the principle as the best means of carrying out the command of Christ, "Take no thought for the morrow, for the morrow shall take thought for itself." Allow me to recommend this asylum to your liberality as a refuge in adversity for those who were careful in prosperity. It is a quiet retreat for decayed members of Benefit Societies, and I am sorry to inform you that many of its rooms are vacant, not from want of candidates, but from a lack of funds. It is a pity that so much public property should be unemployed. Help the committee then to use the houses.

And, now, in concluding, let me remind the Christian that there is one thing he has not to do, and that is, he has not to provide salvation, nor grace, nor sustenance, nor promises for tomorrow. No, beloved; but we often talk as if we had. We say, "How shall I persevere through such and such a trial?" "Sufficient unto the day is the evil thereof." You must not boast of today's grace as though it were enough for tomorrow. But you need not be afraid. With tomorrow's difficulties there will be tomorrow's help; with tomorrow's foes, tomorrow's friends; with tomorrow's dangers, tomorrow's preservations. Let us look forward, then, to tomorrow as a thing we have not to provide for in spiritual matters, for the atonement is finished, the covenant ratified, and therefore every promise shall be fulfilled, and be "yea and amen" to us, not only in one tomorrow, but in fifty thousand tomorrows, if so many could run over our heads.

And now just let us utter the words of the text again, very solemnly and earnestly. O young men in all your glory! O maidens in all your beauty! "Boast not yourselves of tomorrow." The worm may be at your cheeks very soon. O strong men whose bones are full of marrow! O you mighty men, whose nerves seem of brass, and your sinews of steel! "Boast not of tomorrow." "How'l, fir tree," for cedars have fallen before now. Though you think yourselves great, God can pull you down. Above all, you gray heads, "Boast not yourselves of tomorrow," with one foot hanging over the unfathomable gulf of eternity, and the other just tottering on the edge of time! I beseech you do not boast yourselves of tomorrow. In truth I do believe that gray heads are not less foolish on this point than very childhood. I remember reading a story of a man who wanted to buy his neighbor's farm next to him. He went to him and asked him whether he would sell it. He said, "No, I will not." So he went home and said, "Never mind, Farmer So-and-so is an old man. When he is dead, I shall buy it." The man was seventy and his neighbor sixty-eight. He thought the other would be sure to die before him. It is often so with men. They are making schemes that will only walk over their graves when they will not feel them. The winds shall soon howl across the green sward that covers their tomb, but they shall not hear its wailing. Take care of the "todays." Look not through the glass of futurity, but look at the things of today. "Boast not thyself of tomorrows; for thou knowest not what a day may bring forth."

11

The Best Friend

Thine own friend, and thy father's friend, forsake not (Proverbs 27:10).

True friends are very scarce. We have a great many acquaintances, and sometimes we call them friends, and so misuse the noble word "friendship." Peradventure, in some after day of adversity, when these so-called friends have looked out for their own interests and left us to do the best we can for ourselves, that word friendship may come back to us with sad and sorrowful associations. The friend in need is the friend indeed, and such friends, I say again, are scarce. When you have found such a man and proved the sincerity of his friendship, when he has been faithful to your father and to you, grapple him to yourself with hooks of steel and never let him go. It may be that because he is a faithful friend, he will sometimes vex you and anger you. See how Solomon puts it in this very chapter: "Open rebuke is better than secret love. Faithful are the wounds of a friend." It takes a great deal of friendship to be able to tell a man of his faults. It is no friendship that flatters. It is small friendship that holds its tongue when it ought to speak. But it is true friendship that can speak at the right time, and, if need be, even speak so sharply as to cause a wound. If you are like many other foolish folk, you will be angry with the man who is so much your friend that he will tell you the truth. If you are unworthy of your friend, you will begin to grow weary of him when he is performing on your behalf the most heroic act of pure charity by warning you of your danger and reminding you of your imperfection. Solomon, in prospect of such a case, knowing that this is one of the greatest trials of friendship among such poor imperfect beings as we are, tells us not to forsake, for this reason—nor indeed, for any other reason—the man

This sermon was taken from *The Metropolitan Tabernacle Pulpit* and was preached on Thursday evening, February 23, 1882.

who has been to us and to our family a true friend: "Thine own friend, and thy father's friend, forsake not."

I do not think that I should waste your time if I were to give you a lecture upon friendship—its duties, its dangers, its rights, and its privileges—but it is not my intention to do so. There is one Friend to whom these words of Solomon are specially applicable. There is a Friend who is the chief and highest of all friends. When I speak of Him, I feel that I am not spiritualizing the text in the least. He is a true and real Friend, and these words are truly and really applicable to Him. If ever the text is emphatic, it is so when it is applied to him, for there was never such another friend to us and to our fathers. There is no friend to whom we ought to be so intensely attached as to Him: "Thine own friend, and thy father's friend, forsake not."

I want, under the guidance of the Holy Spirit, to speak upon this subject thus. First, here is *a descriptive title* which may be fitly applied to Christ by very many of us—He is our own Friend, and also our father's Friend. Secondly, here is *suggestive advice* concerning this Friend: "Forsake him not." And before I have done, I shall say a little upon *a consequent resolution.* I hope that we shall turn the text into a solemn resolve and say, "My own Friend, and my father's Friend, I will not forsake."

A Descriptive Title

First, he is *a Friend,* the Friend of man. I know that Young calls him the "great Philanthropist." I do not care to see that title used just so. It is not good enough for him, though truly the great Lover of man is Christ. Better still is the title which was given to him when he was upon earth, "the Friend of sinners."

> Friend of sinners, is his name.

Their Friend—thinking of them with love when no other eye pitied them and no other heart seemed to care for them. Their Friend— entering in most tender sympathy into the case of the lost, for "the Son of man came to seek and to save that which was lost." Their Friend— giving them good and sound advice and wholesome counsel, for whosoever listens to the words of Christ shall find in His teaching and in His guidance the highest wisdom. Their Friend, however, giving far more than sympathy and mere words—giving a lifetime of holy service for the sake of those whose cause He had espoused, and going further even than this, doing for them the utmost that a friend can do—for what is there more than that a man should lay down his life for his friend? Friend of man, and therefore born of man. Friend of sinners, and therefore living among them and ministering to them. Friend of sinners, and therefore taking their sin upon Himself and bearing it "in his own body on the tree," so fulfilling Gabriel's prophecy that He would come "to finish the transgression, and to make an end of sins, and to make reconciliation for iniquity, and to bring in everlasting righteousness."

Christ has done for us all that needed to be done. He has done much more than we ever could have asked Him to do or expected Him to do. He has done more for us than we can understand even now that He has done it, and more than you and I are likely ever to understand even when our intellect shall have been developed and enlarged to the utmost degree before the eternal throne. Even there I do not think we shall ever fully know how much we owe to the friendship of our best Friend. However self-denying and tender other friends may be, our Lord must ever stand at the head of the list, and we will not put a second there as worthy of any comparison with Him.

It is a very blessed thing, next, to have the Lord Jesus Christ as having been our father's Friend. There are some of us to whom this has been literally true for many generations. I suppose that there is some pride in being the fourteenth earl, or the tenth duke, or having a certain rank among men. But, sometimes, quietly to myself, I glory in my pedigree because I can trace the line of spiritual grace back as far as I can go to men who loved the Lord, and who, many of them, have preached His Word. Many of you, I know, in this church and in other churches have a glorious heraldry in the line of the Lord's nobles. It is true that some of you have had the great mercy of being taken like trees out of the desert and planted in the courts of our God, for which you may well be glad. But others of you are slips from vines that, in their turn, were slips from other vines loved and cared for by the great Husbandman. You cannot tell how long this blessed succession has continued. Your fathers, and your fathers' fathers, as far back as you can trace them, were friends of Christ. Happy Ephraim, whose father Joseph had God with him! Happy Joseph, whose father Jacob saw God at Bethel! Happy Jacob, whose father Isaac walked in the fields and meditated in communion with Jehovah! Happy Isaac, whose father Abraham had spoken with God and was called "the friend of God." God has a habit of loving families. David said, "The mercy of the Lord is from everlasting to everlasting upon them that fear him, and his righteousness unto children's children; to such as keep his covenant, and to those that remember his commandments to do them." Grace does not run in the blood, but often the stream of divine mercy has run side by side with it. Instead of the fathers have been the children, whom the Lord has made to be princes in the earth.

Some of you, perhaps, have fathers and mothers still living whose example you may fitly follow. I charge you, never forsake your father's

God, or, what is more tender still, the God of your mother. Others of you have parents in heaven. Well, they are still yours, that sacred relationship is not broken. You remember your mother's last grasp of your hand when she bade you follow her to heaven. You recollect your father's appeals to you, in his long sickness, when he pleaded with you to take heed to your ways and not neglect the things of God, but seek him in the days of your youth. Well, did you ever hear your father say anything against his God? Did your mother ever, in her confiding moments, whisper in your ear, "Mary, do not trust in God, for He has betrayed your mother's confidence"? No; I know they did not talk like that, for He was their best Friend. He who was such a Friend to the dear old man whom you can never forget, He who cheered the heart of that gracious matron whose sweet face rises before you now—oh, I beseech you, forsake Him not! "Thine own friend, and thy father's friend, forsake not."

Still, the sweetest part of the text lies in these words, *"Thine own friend."* I do not think that I can preach on those words. I can take them in my mouth, and they are like honey for sweetness, but they must be personally enjoyed to be fully appreciated. There are some precious lines we sometimes sing—

> The health is of my countenance,
> Yea, mine own God is he—

which exactly describe the blessedness of "thine own friend."

Now, if it be true that Christ is your own Friend, then you have spoken with Him, you have held sweet converse with Him, you have placed your confidence in Him, you have told Him your lost estate and sinfulness, and you have reposed in Him as your own Savior. You have put your cause into His hands, and you have left it there. If He be indeed your own Friend, then He has helped you. You were a stranger, and He has taken you in. You were naked, and He has clothed you. You were spiritually sick and in prison, and He came to you and healed you. Yes, and He wore your chains and bade you go free. He took your sicknesses and bade you take His health, and so He made you whole. Aye, and He restored you even from the grave, and went into that grave Himself that by His death, you might live. You know that it is so. Day by day you keep up communion with Him. You could not live without Him, for He is such a Friend to you, and thou dost rest on him with all thy weight as thou comest up from the wilderness with him, leaning on thy Beloved, "thine own friend."

Now is the friendship all on one side, though your side is a very little one. You would make it greater if it were in your power, for you have confessed His name, you have united yourself with His people, you love to join with them in prayer and praise. You are not ashamed to be called by Christ's name as a Christian or to speak well of that name, and you desire to consecrate to Him all that you have. Better than all this, while you do call Him Friend, He also calls you friend, as He said to His disciples, "Ye are my friends, if ye do whatsoever I command you." Dare I say the words, yet, dare I doubt the truth of the words— Jesus is *my* Friend? There is one we read of in the Bible who was David's captain of the host and another who was David's counselor, but there was one man whom we always call "David's friend, Jonathan." I envy him such a title. Yet Jesus gives this name to all those who come and put their trust in Him and so find Him to be their Friend.

Now, inasmuch as the Lord Jesus is "thine own friend, and thy fathers friend," the injunction of the text comes to you with peculiar force: "Forsake him not." Can you forsake Him? Look at His face, all red with bloody sweat for you, nor His face alone, for He is covered all over with that gory robe wherein He wrought out your redemption. He that works for bread must sweat, but He that worked for your eternal life did sweat great drops of blood falling down to the ground. Can you forsake Him? He stands at Pilate's bar, He is mocked by Herod's men of war, He is scourged by Pilate, and all for you. Can you forsake Him? He goes up to the cross of Calvary, and the cruel iron is driven through His hands and feet. There He makes expiation for your guilt. He is your Friend, even to the ignominy of a felon's death. Can you forsake Him? He lays His pierced hand on you, and He says, "Will you also go away?" Or, as He worded it to the Twelve, "Ye also will not go away, will you?" So it might be read: "Many of my supposed friends have gone, and so have proved themselves to be, not friends, but traitors; but ye also will not go away, will you?" And He seems to make an appeal to them with those tearful, tender eyes of His—"as the eyes of doves by the rivers of waters, washed with milk, and fitly set"—"Ye also will not go away, will you?"

And when you turn your eye another way and think not merely of the shame your Friend endured for you, but recollect what is an equal proof of His love that He is not ashamed of you now that He is in His glory. That, amidst the throng of angels and cherubim and seraphim that frequent His courts above, He does not disdain to know that He is the brother of these poor earthworms down below, for even there He wears the body which proves Him to be our next of kin. Aye, He wears the scars which proved that for us He endured the death penalty itself, and even now He is not ashamed to call us brothers and sisters.

As you think of all this, can you forsake Him? Because you are somewhat better off than you once were, will you leave the little gathering of poor folk with whom you used to worship so happily, and will you go to some more fashionable place where there is music, but little of the music of the name of Jesus. Or will you go where there is gorgeous architecture, it may be, and masquerading and mummery, and I know not what, but little of the sweet savor of His presence and the dropping of that dew which He always brings with Him wherever He comes? Oh, it is a pity—it is a sorrowful pity, it is a meanness that would disgrace a mere worldling—when a man, who once confessed Christ and followed Him, must needs turn his back upon his Lord because his own coat is made of better material than it used to be, and his balance at the bank is heavier!

I had almost said—Then let the Judas go, be his own place what it may—it were almost a dishonor to Christ to wish the traitor back. Oh, will you go away, either from the Crucified or from the Glorified, for if you will forsake this Friend, "Behold, he cometh!" Every hour brings Him nearer. The chariots of His glory have glowing axles, and you may almost hear them as they speed toward us. Then what will you do when you have forsaken your own Friend and your father's Friend, and you hear Him say, "I never knew you; I never knew you"? God grant that it may never be the lot of any of us here present to hear those awful words!

Suggestive Advice

There is, to me, in the text, a suggestion which the text itself does not suggest. That is to say, *it suggests something by not suggesting it.* The text does not suggest to me that my own Friend and my father's Friend will ever forsake me. It seems to hint that I may forsake Him, but it does not suggest that He will ever forsake me, and He never will do so. If the Lord had ever meant to forsake me, He has had so many good reasons for doing it, that He would have done it long ago. The apostle says of those who are journeying to the better country that, "if they had been mindful of that country from whence they came out, they might have had opportunity to have returned." Certainly, our blessed Lord and Master, if He had desired to leave us to perish, had many an opportunity to return to heaven before He died. Since then, He has had many occasions when He might have said, "I really must withdraw my friendship from you," if He had ever wished to do so. But His love is constant to its line: "Having loved his own which were in the world, he loved them unto the end." His is a friendship which never changes. You shall never fall back on Him and find that He has withdrawn the arm with which He formerly upheld you. You shall find, in life and in death, that "there is a friend that sticketh closer than a brother." Let us be cheered by the assurance that He will never forsake us.

Now let us go on to what the text does suggest in so many words. It suggests to us the question, *In what sense can we forsake Christ?* Well, there is more than one sense in which a man may forsake Christ. Two passages rise to my mind at this moment: "Then all the disciples forsook him, and fled." That was one sort of forsaking. They were all afraid and ran away from their Lord in the hour of His betrayal into the hands of sinners. But it is quite another kind of forsaking when we read: "From that time many of his disciples went back, and walked no more with him." The first forsaking was the result of a sudden fear, much to be deplored and very blameworthy, but still only temporary in its effects. The other was the deliberate act of those who, in cool blood, refused to accept Jesus Christ's doctrine or to follow Him any farther, and so turned back and walked no more with Him. This last forsaking is incurable. The former one was cured almost as soon as the sudden fear that caused it was removed. For we find John and even Peter following the Master to the judgment hall, and the whole of the disciples soon gathered around Him after His resurrection.

I would say to you, dear friend, "Thine own friend, and thy father's friend, forsake not" in any sense at all. Forsake Him not even in your moments of alarm. Pray God that then you may play the man, and not forsake Him and flee. And then, in the other sense, let no quarrel ever arise between you and Christ's most precious truth, so as to lead you deliberately to leave Him, for this is the worst of all kinds of forsaking. If we never forsake Him in any sense at all, then it is quite certain that we shall never forsake Him in the worst sense. I remember a little merriment I had with a good Wesleyan brother, the clerk of the works, when the Tabernacle was being built. He wanted me to go up a ladder right into those lantern lights. I said, "No, thank you; I would rather not." "But," he replied, "I thought you had no fear of falling." "Yes," I answered, "that is quite true. I have no fear of finally falling away. But the belief that the Lord will preserve me does not exercise any evil influence over me, for it keeps me from running unnecessary risks by climbing up ladders. But you good brethren, who are so afraid of falling, do not seem to show it practically in your conduct, for you go up and down the ladders as nimbly as possible."

I have sometimes met with persons who think that if we believe that we shall never fall so as to perish, we are apt to become presumptuous. But we do not, dear friends. There are other truths that come in to balance this one, so that what they think might come of it is by God's good grace prevented. I am not quite sure that those who think that they may finally fall and perish are sufficiently impressed with that belief so as to be always careful. The fact is, that your carefulness of walk does not depend merely upon your view of this doctrine or that. But it does depend upon your state of heart, and a great many other things besides, so that you have no reason to judge what you might do if you believed such-and-such a truth. Because if you did believe it, perhaps you would at the same time be a better man, and the possibility that appears to linger around the doctrine would vanish so far as you are concerned. Let this be the language of all of us who love the Lord as we look up confidently and reverently to Him—

> We have no fear that thou shouldst lose
> One whom eternal love could choose;
> But we would ne'er this grace abuse,
> Let us not fall. Let us not fall.

I know that, if we are truly the Lord's, He will not suffer us to forsake Him. But I must have a wholesome fear lest I should forsake Him, for who am I that I should be sure that I have not deceived myself? And I may have done so. After all, I may forsake Him after the loudest professions, and even after the greatest apparent sincerity in avowing that I never will turn away from Him.

So, I ask again: In what sense can we forsake our Lord? Well, there are many senses, but perhaps you will see better what I mean if I describe *the general process of forsaking a friend*. I hope that you have never had to undergo it. I do not know that I ever had. But, still, I can imagine that it is something like this. The old gentleman was your father's friend; he also had been your own friend and has done you many a good turn. But, at last, he has said something which has provoked you to anger, or he has done something which you have misunderstood or misinterpreted. Now you feel very cool toward him when you meet. You pass the time of day, and perhaps say very much the same things which you used to say, but they are said in a very different fashion. Now, that is how we begin to forsake our God. We may keep up the appearance of friendship with Christ, but it is a very cool affair. We go to a place of worship, but there is no enjoyment, no enthusiasm, no earnestness.

Then the next thing is, that you do not call to see your friend as frequently as you used to do. It has not come to an open rupture between you, so you do look in at certain set times when you are expected. But there are none of those little flying visits and that popping in upon him unawares just to get a look at his face as you used to do. And, on his part, he does not come to see you much. And that is how our forsaking of Christ generally continues. We do not go to talk with Him as we once did, and when we do go to His house, we find that He is not at home. "Can two walk together, except they be agreed?"

Then, by-and-by, perhaps there is a sharp word spoken, and your friend feels that you do not want him. You have said something that cuts him to the quick, and grieves him. It was not anything so very bad if it had been spoken to a stranger. But to be said to him who was your father's friend, to him whom you always expected to come in and whom you loved to see—to say it to him was very hard, and he naturally took umbrage at it. That is how it comes to pass between Christ and professors. There is something done which might not be of so much account in the case of nonprofessors or the openly ungodly. But it is very bad in one who professed to have Christ for his Friend.

And do you know what happens, by-and-by, when your friend is being discarded? At last, he does not call at all, and you do not go to see him. Perhaps the breach is still further widened, and little presents are sent back or treated with contempt. There is that oil painting which your father would have, though he could scarcely afford it, because he loved his friend so much, and which he hung up in so conspicuous a place in his house. Well, the other day, the string broke, and you did not buy a fresh piece of cord to hang it up again. In fact, you put the picture away in the lumber room, and you really do not care what becomes of it. The little tokens of past affection are all put away, for there is an open rupture now. When somebody spoke to you about him, lately, you said, "Oh, pray don't mention him to me! He is no friend of mine now. I used to be on intimate terms with him once, but I have altered my opinion about him altogether." So do some professors act toward the Lord Jesus Christ. Those little tokens of love which they thought they had from Him they send back. They do not remain in fellowship with His church. They do all that they possibly can to disown Him. In the meanwhile, the blessed Lord of love is obliged to disown them, too. His church disowns them. By-and-by, the rupture has become complete. May that never be the portion of any of you!

"No," says one, "it never will be." My dear friend, if you are so confident as that, you are the person about whom I am most afraid. I recollect one who used to pray among us, but we had to put him out of the church for evil living. There was one of our members who said that night, "If that man is not a child of God, I am not one myself." I said, "My dear brother, do not talk like that. I would not pit my soul against the soul of any man, for I do know a little of myself, but I do not know other men as well as I know myself." I am very much afraid that neither of the two men I have mentioned was a child of God. By their speech they seemed to be Christians, but their acts were not like those of God's people. It does not do for us to talk as that man did, but to pray to the Lord, "Hold me up, and I shall be safe." That is the proper prayer for us. Or else it may happen even to us as happened to them, and we may forsake our own Friend and our father's Friend.

Now, *what reasons can we possibly have for forsaking Christ?* We ought to do nothing for which we cannot give good reasons. I have known persons who very properly forsake their former friends because they have themselves become new creatures in Christ Jesus. They have rightly and wisely given up the acquaintances with whom they used to sin. They cannot go now to the house where everything is contrary to their feelings. But it is not so with Christ. Some so-called friends drag a man down, lower him, injure him, impose upon him, and at last he is obliged to let them go. But we cannot say that of Christ. His friendship has drawn us up, helped us, sanctified us, elevated us. We owe everything to that friendship. We cannot have a reason, therefore, for forsaking this Friend.

I have known some to outgrow an acquaintance or friend. They really have not been able to continue to have common views and sympathies. While their friend has remained in the mire, they have risen into quite different men by reason of education and other influences. But we can never outgrow Christ; that is not possible. The more we grow in a right sense, the more we shall become like Him. A man who has been the friend of our father and of ourselves is the very man to have still as a friend because he probably understands all about the family difficulties and the family troubles, and he also understands us. Why, he nursed us when we were children, and therefore he knows most about us.

I remember that when lying sore sick I had a letter from a kind old gentleman who said that he had that day celebrated his eightieth birthday, and the choicest friend he had at his dinner table was the old family doctor. He said, "He has attended to me so long that he thoroughly knows my constitution. He is nearly as old as myself. But the first time I was ill I had him, and he has attended me now for forty years. Once," he said, "when I had a severe attack of gout, I was tempted to try some very famous man who very nearly killed me. And until I got back to my old friend, I never was really well again." So he wrote to advise me to get some really good physician, let him know my constitution, to stick to him, and never go off to any of the patent medicines or the quacks of the day.

Oh, but there is a great deal of truth in that in a spiritual sense! With the utmost reverence, we may say that the Lord Jesus Christ has been our family Physician. Did He not attend my father in all his sicknesses, and my grandfather, too? And He knows the ins and outs of my constitution—He knows my ways, good and bad, and all my sorrows. Therefore I do not go to anyone else for relief. I advise you also to keep to Jesus Christ, do not forsake Him. If you ever are tempted to go aside, even for a little while, I pray that you may have grace enough to come back quickly, and to commit yourself again to Him and never go astray again. There is the blessing of having one who is wise, one who is tried, one whose sympathy has been tested, one who has become, as it were, one of your family. There is the blessing of having one who has taken your whole household to his heart, and made it part and parcel of himself. Such a Friend to your own soul, and to your father's soul, forsake not.

Do not forsake Him, dear friends, because I almost tremble to say it—*you will want Him some day.* Even if you would never need Him in the future, you ought not to forsake Him. I do not quite like that verse of the hymn at the end of our hymnbook—

> Ashamed of Jesus! yes, I may,
> When I've no guilt to wash away;
> No tear to wipe, no good to crave,
> No fears to quell, no soul to save.

No, I *may not.* When all my guilt is gone, I shall not be ashamed of Jesus. When I am in heaven and need no more the pardon of sin, I certainly shall not be ashamed of Him who brought me there. No, but I shall glory in Him more than ever. Your friendship to Christ, and mine, ought not to depend upon what we are going to get out of Him. We must love Him now for what He is, for all that He has already done, and for His own blessed person and personal beauties, which every day should hold fast our love and bind us in chains of affection to Him.

But suppose you do think of forsaking Christ, where are you going to get another friend to take His place? You must have a friend of some sort. Who is going to sit in Christ's chair? Whose portrait is to be hung up in the old familiar place when the old Friend is discarded? To whom are you going to tell your griefs, and from whom will you expect to receive help in time of need? Who will be with you in sickness? Who will be with you in the hour of death? Ah! there is no other who can ever fill the vacuum which the absence of Christ would make. Therefore, never forsake Him.

The Consequent Resolve

Let this be your resolve, by His grace, *instead of forsaking Him, you will cleave to Him more closely than ever.* You will own Him when it brings you dishonor to do so. You will trust Him when He wounds you, for "faithful are the wounds of a friend." You will serve Him when it is costly to do it, when it involves self-denial. Resolved that, by the help of His ever-blessed Spirit without whom you can do nothing, you will never, in any sort of company, conceal the fact that you are a Christian. Never, under any possible circumstances, wish to be otherwise than a servant of such a Master, a friend of such a Lord. Come now, dear young friends who are getting cool toward Christ and elder friends to whom religion is becoming monotonous, come to your Lord once more and ask Him to bind you with cords, even with cords to the horns of the altar. You have had time to count the cost of all Egyptia's treasure, forego it and forswear it once for all. But the riches of Christ you can never count, so come and take Him again to be your All-in-all.

Those about to be baptized will feel, I trust—as we shall when we look on—and say, each man and woman for himself or herself—

> 'Tis done! The great transaction's done:
> I am my Lord's, and he is mine.

Nail your colors to the mast. Bear in your body the marks of the Lord Jesus. Aye, let everyone of us who has been baptized into Christ feel that our whole body bears the watermark, for we have been "buried with him by baptism into death." It was not for the putting off of the filthiness of the flesh, but as a declaration that we were dead to the world and quickened into newness of life in Christ Jesus our Savior. So let it be with you, too, dear friends, as you follow your Lord through the water—cling to Him, cleave to Him. "Thine own friend, and thy father's friend, forsake not." May God add His blessing, for our Lord Jesus Christ's sake! Amen.

12

Pride and Humility

Before destruction the heart of man is haughty, and before honour is humility (Proverbs 18:12).

Almost every event has its prophetic prelude. It is an old and common saying, that "coming events cast their shadows before them." The wise man teaches us the same lesson in the verse before us. When destruction walks through the land, it casts its shadow. It is in the shape of pride. When honor visits a man's house, it casts its shadow before it. It is in the fashion of humility. "Before destruction the heart of man is haughty." Pride is as surely the sign of destruction as the change of mercury in the weather glass is the sign of rain, and far more infallibly so than that. "Before honor is humility," even as before the summer sweet birds return to sing in our land. Everything has its prelude. The prelude of destruction is pride, and of honor, humility. There is nothing into which the heart of man so easily falls as pride. Yet there is no vice which is more frequently, more emphatically, and more eloquently condemned in Scripture. Against pride, prophets have lifted up their voices, evangelists have spoken, and teachers have discoursed. Yes, more, the everlasting God has mounted to the very heights of eloquence when He would condemn the pride of man. The full gushing of the Eternal's mighty language has been most gloriously displayed in the condemnation of the pride of human nature.

Perhaps the most eloquent passage of God's Word is to be found toward the conclusion of the book of Job, where, in most splendid strains of unanswerable eloquence, God hides pride from man by utterly confounding him. There is another very eloquent passage in the fourteenth chapter of Isaiah, where the Lord's holy choler seems to have risen up, and His anger to have waxed hot against the pride of man, when He

---

This sermon was taken from *The New Park Street Pulpit* and was preached on Sunday evening, July 15, 1877.

would utterly and effectually condemn it. He says concerning the great and mighty king of Babylon, "Hell from beneath is moved for thee to meet thee at thy coming: it stirreth up the dead for thee, even all the chief ones of the earth; it hath raised up from their thrones of all the kings of the nations. All they shall speak and say unto thee, Art thou also become weak as we? art thou become like unto us? Thy pomp is brought down to the grave, and the noise of thy viols: the worm is spread under thee, and the worms cover thee. How art thou fallen from heaven O Lucifer, son of the morning! how art thou cut down to the ground, which didst weaken the nations! For thou hast said in thine heart, I will ascend into heaven, I will exalt my throne above the stars of God: I will sit also upon the mount of the congregation, in the sides of the north: I will ascend above the heights of the clouds: I will be like the most High. Yet thou shalt be brought down to hell, to the sides of the pit. They that see thee shall narrowly look upon thee, and consider thee, saying, Is this the man that made the earth to tremble, that did shake kingdoms" (vv. 9–16). Mark how God addresses him, describing hell itself as being astonished at his fall, seeing that he had mounted so high. Yet declaring, assuredly, that his height and greatness were nothing to the Almighty, that He would pull him down, even though, like an eagle, he had built his nest among the stars.

I say there is nothing more eloquently condemned in Scripture than pride, and yet there is no trap into which we poor silly birds so easily flee, no pitfall into which, like foolish beasts of the earth, we so continually run. On the other hand, humility is a grace that has many promises given to it in the Scripture. Perhaps most promises are given to faith, and love is often considered to be the brightest of the train of virtues. Yet humility holds by no means an inferior place in God's Word, and there are hundreds of promises linked to it. Every grace seems to be like a nail on which precious blessings hang, and humility has many a mercy suspended from it. "He that exalteth himself shall be abased, and he that humbleth himself shall be exalted." "Blessed are the poor in spirit." In multitudes of other passages, we are reminded that God loves the humble, but that He "bringeth down the mighty from their seats, and exalteth the humble and meek." Now, this morning, we shall have a word to say concerning *pride* and *humility*. May the Holy Spirit preserve us from the one and produce in our hearts the other.

Pride

"Before destruction the heart of man is haughty." Pride, *what is it?* Pride, *where is its seat?* The heart of man. And pride, *what is its consequences?* Destruction.

In the first place, I must try to *describe pride* to you. I might paint it as being the worst malformation of all the monstrous things in creation. It has nothing lovely in it, nothing in proportion, but everything in disorder. It is altogether the very reverse of the creatures that God has made which are pure and holy. Pride, the first-born son of hell, is indeed like its parent, all unclean and vile, and in it there is neither form, fashion, nor comeliness.

In the first place, pride is a *groundless thing*. It stands on the sands. Worse than that, it puts its foot on the billows which yield beneath its tread. Worse still, it stands on bubbles, which soon must burst beneath its feet. Of all things pride has the worst foothold. It has no solid rock on earth whereon to place itself. We have reasons for almost everything, but we have no reasons for pride. Pride is a thing that should be unnatural to us, for we have nothing to be proud of. What is there in man of which he should glory? Our very creation is enough to humble us. What are we but creatures of today? Our frailty should be sufficient to lay us low, for we shall be gone tomorrow. Our ignorance should tend to keep pride from our lips. What are we, but like the wild donkey's colt which knows nothing? And our sins ought effectually to stop our mouths and lay us in the dust. Of all things in the world, pride toward God is that which has the very least excuse. It has neither stick nor stone whereon to build. Yet like the spider, it carries its own web in its bowels and can, of itself, spin that wherewith to catch its prey. It seems to stand upon itself for it has nothing besides whereon it can rest.

Oh! man, learn to reject pride, seeing that you have no reason for it. Whatever you are, you have nothing to make you proud. The more you have, the more you are in debt to God. You should not be proud of that which renders you a debtor. Consider your origin. Look back to the hole of the pit whence you were digged. Consider what you would have been, even now, if it were not for Divine grace. And, consider, that you will yet be lost in hell if grace does not hold you up. Consider that among the damned, there are none that would have been more damned than yourself if grace had not kept you from destruction. Let this consideration humble you that you have nothing whereon to ground your pride.

Again, it is a *brainless thing* as well as a groundless thing, for it brings no profit with it. There is no wisdom in a self-exaltation. Other vices have some excuse, for men seem to gain by them. Avarice, pleasure, lust, have some plea, but the man who is proud sells his soul cheaply. He opens wide the floodgates of his heart to let men see how deep is the flood within his soul. Then suddenly it flows out and all is gone—and all is nothing for one puff of empty wind, one word of sweet applause. The soul is gone and not a drop is left. In almost every other sin, we gather up the ashes when the fire is gone but here, what is left?

The covetous man has his shining gold, but what has the proud man? He has less than he would have had without his pride and is no gainer whatever. Oh! man, if you were as mighty as Gabriel and had all his holiness, still you would be an arrant fool to be proud, for pride would sink you from your angel station to the rank of devils, and bring you from the place where Lucifer, son of the morning, once dwelt, to take up your abode with hideous fiends in perdition.

Pride exalts its head and seeks to honor itself, but it is of all things most despised. It sought to plant crowns upon its brow, and so it has done. But its head was hot, and it put an ice crown there, and it melted all away. Poor pride has decked itself out finely sometimes. It has put on its most gaudy apparel and said to others, "How brilliant I appear!" But, ah! pride, like a harlequin, dressed in your bright colors, you are all the more fool for that. You are but a gazing stock for fools less foolish than yourself. You have no crown as you think you have, nothing solid and real, all is empty and vain. If you, O man, desire shame, be proud. A monarch has waded through slaughter to a throne and shut the gates of mercy on mankind to win a little glory. But when he has exalted himself and has been proud, worms have devoured him, like Herod, or have devoured his empire until it passed away, and with it his pride and glory. Pride wins no crown. Men never honor it, not even the menial slaves of earth. For all men look down on the proud man and think him less than themselves.

Again, pride is *the maddest thing* that can exist. It feeds upon its own vitals. It will take away its own life, that with its blood it may make a purple for its shoulders. It saps and undermines its own house that it may build its pinnacles a little higher, and then the whole structure tumbles down. Nothing proves men so mad as pride. For this they have given up rest, ease, and repose to find rank and power among men. For this they have dared to risk their hope of salvation—to leave the gentle yoke of Jesus, and go toiling wearily along the way of life— seeking to save themselves by their own works, and at last to stagger into the mire of fell despair. Oh! man, hate pride, flee from it, abhor it, let it not dwell with you. If you want to have a madman in your heart, embrace pride, for you shall never find one more mad than he.

Then pride is a *protean thing*. It changes its shape. It is all forms in the world. You may find it in any fashion you may choose. You may see it in the beggar's rags as well as in the rich man's garment. It dwells with the rich and with the poor. The man without a shoe to his foot may be as proud as if he were riding in a chariot. Pride can be found in every rank of society—among all classes of men. Sometimes it is an Arminian and talks about the power of the creature. Then it turns Calvinist and boasts of its fancied security—forgetful of the Maker who alone can keep our faith alive. Pride can profess any form of religion. It may be a Quaker and wear no collar to its coat. It may be a Churchman and worship God in splendid cathedrals. It may be a Dissenter and go to the common meeting house. It is one of the most Catholic things in the world. It attends all kinds of chapels and churches. Go where you will, you will see pride. It comes up with us to the house of God. It goes with us to our houses. It is found on the mart and the exchange, in the streets and everywhere.

Let me hint at one or two of the forms which it assumes. Sometimes pride takes the doctrinal shape. It teaches the doctrine of self-sufficiency. It tells us what man can do and will not allow that we are lost, fallen, debased, and ruined creatures as we are. It hates divine sovereignty and rails at election. Then if it is driven from that, it takes another form. It allows that the doctrine of free grace is true but does not feel it. It acknowledges that salvation is of the Lord alone, but still it prompts men to seek heaven by their own works, even by the deeds of the law. And when driven from that, it will persuade men to join something with Christ in the matter of salvation. When that is all rent up and the poor rag of our righteousness is all burned, pride will get into the Christian's heart as well as the sinner's. It will flourish under the name of self-sufficiency, teaching the Christian that he is "rich and increased in goods, having need of nothing." It will tell him that he does not need daily grace, that past experience will do for tomorrow, that he knows enough, toils enough, prays enough. It will make him forget that he has "not yet attained." It will not allow him to press forward to the things that are before, forgetting the things that are behind. It enters into his heart and tempts the believer to set up an independent business for himself, and until the Lord brings about a spiritual bankruptcy, pride will keep him from going to God.

Pride has ten thousand shapes. It is not always that stiff and starched gentleman that you picture. It is a vile, creeping, insinuating thing that will twist itself like a serpent into our hearts. It will talk of humility, and prate about being dust and ashes. I have known men talk about their corruption most marvelously, pretending to be all humility, while at the same time they were the proudest wretches that could be found this side the gulf of separation. Oh! my friends, you cannot tell how many shapes pride will assume. Look sharp about you or you will be deceived by it, and when you think you are entertaining angels, you will find you have been receiving devils unawares.

Now, I have to speak of *the seat of pride*—the heart. The true throne of pride everywhere is the heart of man. If, my dear friends, we desire by God's grace to put down pride, the only way is to begin with the heart. Now let me tell your a parable in the form of an eastern story which will set this truth in its proper light. A wise man in the east, called a dervish, in his wanderings came suddenly upon a mountain, and he saw beneath his feet a smiling valley in the midst of which there flowed a river. The sun was shining on the stream, and the water as it reflected the sunlight looked pure and beautiful. When he descended, he found it was muddy, and the water utterly unfit for drinking. Nearby he saw a young man in the dress of a shepherd who was with much diligence filtering the water for his flocks. At one moment he placed some water into a pitcher, and then allowing it to stand; after it had settled, he poured the clean fluid into a cistern. Then, in another place, he would be seen turning aside the current for a little, and letting it ripple over the sand and stones that it might be filtered and the impurities removed. The dervish watched the young man endeavoring to fill a large cistern with clear water. He said to him, "My son, why all this toil? What purpose do you answer by it?" The young man replied, "Father, I am a shepherd. This water is so filthy that my flock will not drink of it. Therefore, I am obliged to purify it little by little so I collect enough in this way that they may drink, but it is hard work." So saying, he wiped the sweat from his brow, for he was exhausted with his toil. "Right well have you labored," said the wise man, "but do you know your toil is not well applied? With half the labor you might attain a better end. I should conceive that the source of this stream must be impure and polluted. Let us take a pilgrimage together and see."

They then walked some miles, climbing their way over many a rock, until they came to a spot where the stream took its rise. When they came near to it, they saw flocks of wild fowls flying away, and wild beasts of the earth rushing into the forest. These had come to drink and had soiled the water with their feet. They found an open well which kept continually flowing, but by reason of these creatures, which perpetually disturbed it, the stream was always turbid and muddy. "My son," said the wise man, "set to work now to protect the fountain and guard the well, which is the source of this stream, and when you have done that, if you can keep these wild beasts and fowl away, the stream will flow of itself, all pure and clear, and you will have no longer need for your toil." The young man did it, and as he labored, the wise man said to him, "My son, hear the word of wisdom. If you are wrong, seek not to correct your outward life, but seek first to get your heart correct, for out of it are the issues of life. Your life shall be pure when once your heart is so." So if we would get rid of pride, we should not proceed to arrange our dress by adopting some special costume, or to qualify our language by using an outlandish tongue. But let us seek of God that He would purify our hearts from pride, and then assuredly if pride is purged from the heart, our life also shall be humble. Make the tree good, and then the fruit shall be good. Make the fountain pure, and the stream shall be sweet. Oh! that God might grant us all, by His grace, that our hearts may be kept with diligence, so that pride may never enter there lest we be haughty in our hearts and find that afterward comes wrath.

This brings me to the other point, which is, *the consequence of pride*—destruction, a fact which we can prove by hundreds of instances in Scripture. When men have become proud, destruction has come upon them. See you yon bright angel chanting the loud anthem of praise before his Maker's throne? Can anything tarnish that angel's glory, rob him of his harp, despoil him of his crown? Yes, see there enters a destroyer whose name is pride. He assaults the angel, and his harp strings are snapped in twain. His crown is taken from his brow, and his glory is departed. Yon falling spirit descending into hell is he who once was Lucifer, son of the morning. He has now become Father of nights, even the Lord of Darkness, Satan, the Fallen one.

See you again that happy pair walking in the midst of luscious fruits, and flowery walks and bowers of Paradise? Can anything spoil Eden and ruin those happy beings? Yes, pride comes in the shape of a serpent and asks them to seek to be as gods. They eat of the forbidden fruit, and pride withers their paradise and blasts their Eden. Out they go to till the ground whence they were taken to beget and to bring forth us who are their children—sons of toil and sorrow. Do you see that man after God's own heart continually singing his Maker's praise? Can anything make him sad? Can you suppose that he shall ever be laid prostrate on the earth, groaning and crying and asking "that the bones which God hath broken may rejoice?" Yes, pride can do that. It will pit into his heart that he will number his people, that he will count the tribes of Israel, to show how great and mighty is his empire. It is done, and a terrible pestilence sweeps over his land on account of his pride. Let David's aching heart show how destruction comes to a man's glory when he once begins to make a god of it. See that other good and holy man who, like David, was much after God's own heart. He is rich and increased in goods. The Babylonian ambassadors are come, and he shows them all he has. Do you not hear that threatening, "Thy treasures shall be carried away, and thy sons and thy daughters shall be servants to the king of Babylon?" The destruction of Hezekiah's wealth must come because he is proud thereof.

But for the most notable instance of all, let me show you yonder palace, perhaps the most magnificent which has even yet been built. In it there walks one who, lifting up his head on high as if he were more than mortal man, exclaims, "See ye this great Babylon that I have builded?" Oh! pride, what have you done? You have more power than a wizard's wand! Mark the mighty builder of Babylon creeping on the earth. Like oxen he is devouring grass. His nails have grown like birds' claws, his hair like eagles' feathers, and his heart has gone from him. Pride did all that, that it might be fulfilled which God has written, "Before destruction the heart of man is haughty."

Is your heart haughty, sinner this morning? Do you despise God's sovereignty? Will you not submit yourself to Christ's yoke? Do you seek to weave a righteousness of your own? Are you seeking to be or to do something? Are you desirous of being great and mighty in your own esteem? Hear me then, sinner, destruction is coming upon you. As truly as ever you exalt yourself, you shall be abased. Your *destruction,* in the fullest and blackest sense of the word, is hurrying on to overwhelm you. And oh! Christian, is your heart haughty this morning? Have you come here glorying in your graces? Are you proud of yourself, that you have had such high frames and such sweet experiences? Mark you, brother or sister, there is a destruction coming to you also. Some of your proud things will be pulled up by the roots, some of your graces will be shattered, and your good works, perhaps, will become loathsome to you, and you will abhor yourself in dust and ashes. As truly as ever you exalt yourself, there will be a destruction come to you, O saint—the destruction of yourself. There will be a destruction come to you, O saint—the destruction of your joys and of your comforts, though there can be no destruction of your soul.

Pride, you know, is most likely to meet with destruction because it is too tall to walk upright. It is most likely to tumble down, because it is always looking upward in its ambition, and never looks to its feet. There only needs to be a pitfall in the way, or even a stone, and down it goes. It is sure to tumble because it is never contented with being where it is. It is always seeking to be climbing, and boys that will climb must expect to fall. Pride is foolhardy and will venture upon scaling any rock. Sometimes it holds on by a brier and that pricks it. Sometimes it holds on by a flint and that cuts it. There it goes, toiling and laboring on until it gets as high as it can, and then, from its very height, it is likely to fall. Nature itself tells us to avoid high things. Who is he that can stand upon an eminence without a reeling brain and without a temptation to cast himself down? Pride, when most successful, stands in slippery places. Who would choose to dwell on a pinnacle of the temple? That is where pride has built its house, and verily it seems but natural that pride should down if pride will up. God will carry out this saying, "Before destruction, the heart of man is haughty." Yet beloved, I am persuaded that all I can say to you or to myself can never keep pride from us. The Lord alone can bolt the door of the heart against pride. Pride is like the flies of Egypt, all Pharaoh's soldiers could not keep them out. I am sure all the strong resolutions and devout aspirations we may have cannot keep pride out unless the Lord God Almighty sends a strong wind of His Holy Spirit to sweep it away.

Humility

"Before honor is humility." So then, you see our heavenly Father does not say that we are not to have honor. He has not forbidden it. He has only forbidden us to be proud of it. A good man may have honor in this life. Daniel had honor before the people. Joseph rode in the second chariot, and the people bowed the knee before him. God often clothes His children with honor in the face of their adversaries and makes the wicked confess that the Lord is with them in deed and in truth. But God forbids our making that honor a cloak for pride and bids us seek humility which always accompanies as well as precedes true honor.

Now let us briefly inquire, in the first place, *what is humility?* The best definition I have ever met with is, "to think rightly of ourselves." Humility is to make a right estimate of oneself. It is no humility for a man to think less of himself than he ought, though it might rather puzzle him to do that. Some persons, when they know they can do a thing, tell you they cannot. But you do not call that humility? A man is asked to take part in some meeting. "No," he says, "I have no ability." Yet, if you were to say so yourself he would be offended at you. It is not humility for a man to stand up and depreciate himself and say he cannot do this, that, or the other, when he knows that he is lying. If God gives a man a talent, do you think the man does not know it? If a man has ten talents he has no right to be dishonest to his Maker and to say, "Lord, thou hast only given me five." It is not humility to underrate ourselves. Humility is to think of yourself, if you can, as God thinks of you. It is to feel that if we have talents, God has given them to us, and let it be seen that, like freight in a vessel, they tend to sink us low. The more we have, the lower we ought to lie. Humility is not to say, "I have not this gift," but it is to say, "I have the gift, and I must use it for my Master's glory. I must never seek any honor for myself, for what have I that I have not received?" but, beloved, humility is to feel ourselves lost, ruined, and undone. To be killed by the same hand which, afterward, makes us alive to be ground to pieces as to our own doings and willings, to know and trust in none but Jesus, to be brought to feel and sing—

> Nothing in my hands I bring,
> Simply to thy cross I cling.

Humility is to feel that we have no power of ourselves, but that it all comes from God. Humility is to lean on our Beloved, to believe that He has trodden the winepress alone, to lie on His bosom and slumber sweetly there, to exalt Him, and think less than nothing of ourselves. It is in fact, to annihilate self and to exalt the Lord Jesus Christ as all in all.

Now, what is *the seat or throne of humility?* The throne of humility must be the heart. I do hate, of all things, that humility which lives in the face. There are some persons who always seem to be so very humble when you are with them, but you can discover there is something underneath it all. When they are in some other society, they will brag and say how you told them your whole heart. Take heed of the men who allow you to lay your head in their lap and betray you into the hands of the Philistines. I have met with such persons. I remember a man who used to pray with great apparent humility, and then would go and abuse the servants and make a noise with all his farming men. He was the stiffest and proudest man in the church. Yet he invariably used to tell the Lord in prayer that he was nothing but dust and ashes, that he laid his hand on his lip and his mouth in the dust, and cried, "Unclean, unclean." Indeed he talked of himself in the most despairing way, but I am sure if God had spoken to him, He must have said, "O, you that lie before My throne, you say this, but you do not feel it. For you will go your way and take your brother by the throat, exalt yourself above all your fellow-creatures, and be a very Diotrephes in the church, and a Herod in the world." I dislike that humility which rests in outward things. There is a kind of oily, sanctimonious, proud humility, which is not the genuine article, though it is sometimes extremely like it. You may be deceived by it once or twice, but by-and-by you discover that is a wolf dexterously covered with sheep's clothing. It arrays itself in the simplest dress in the world. It talks in the gentlest and humblest style. It says, "We must not intrude our own peculiar sentiments, but must always walk in love and charity." But after all, what is it? It is charitable to all except those who hold God's truth, and it is humble to all when it is forced to be humble. It is like one of whom, I dare say, you have read in your childish books—

> So, stooping down, as needs he must
> Who cannot stand upright.

True humility does not continually talk about "dust and ashes," and prate about its infirmities, but it *feels* all that which others say, for it possesses an inwrought feeling of its own nothingness.

Very likely the most humble man in the world won't bend to anybody. John Knox was a truly humble man, yet if you had seen him march before Queen Mary with the Bible in his hand to reprove her, you would have rashly said, "What a proud man!"

Cringing men that bow before everybody are truly proud men. But humble men are those who think themselves so little, they do not think it worthwhile to stoop to serve themselves. Shadrach, Meshach, and Abednego were humble men, for they did not think their lives were worth enough to save them by a sin. Daniel was a humble man; he did not think his place, his station, his whole self worth enough to save them by leaving off prayer. Humility is a thing which must be genuine. The imitation of it is the nearest thing in the world to pride. Seek of God, dear friends, the gift of true humility. Seek to have that breaking in pieces by the Holy Spirit, that breaking in the mortar with the pestle which God Himself gives to His children. Seek that every twig of His rod may drive pride out of you, so that by the blueness of your wound, your soul may be made better. Seek of Him, if He does not show you the chambers of imagery within your own heart that He may take you to Calvary and that He may show you His brightness and His glory, that you may be humble before Him. Never ask to be a mean, cringing, fawning thing. Ask God to make you a man—those are scarce things now-a-days—who only fears God, who knows no fear of any other kind. Do not give yourselves up to any man's power, guidance, or rule, but ask of God that you may have that humility toward Him which gives you the noble bearing of a Christian before others.

Some think that ministers are proud when they resent any interference with their ministry. I consider they would be proud if they allowed it for the sake of peace, which is only another word for their own self-seeking. It is a great mercy when God gives a man to be free from everybody, when he can go into his pulpit careless of what others may think of him. I conceive that a minister should be like a lighthouse keeper. He is out at sea, and nobody can suggest to him that he had better light his candles a little later or anything of the kind. He knows his duty, and he keeps his lamps burning. If he were to follow the opinions of the people on shore, his light might be extinguished altogether. It is a merciful providence that they cannot get to him, so he goes on easily, obeys his regulations as he reads them, and cares little for other people's interpretation. So a minister should not be a weathercock that is turned by the wind, but he should be one who turns the wind. He should not be one who is ruled by others, but one who knows how to stand firm and fast, and keep his light burning, trusting always in God. The minister should believe that if God has raised him up, He will not desert him, but will teach him by His Holy Spirit without the ever-changing advice of men.

Now, in the last place, *what comes of humility?* "Before honor is humility." Humility is the herald which ushers in the great king. It walks before honor, and he who has humility will have honor afterward. I will only apply this spiritually. Have you been brought today to feel that in yourself you are less than nothing and vanity? Are you humbled in the sight of God to know your own unworthiness, your fallen estate in Adam, and the ruin you have brought upon yourself by your own sins? Have you been brought to feel yourself incapable of working out your own salvation unless God shall work in you to will and to do of His own good pleasure? Have you been brought to say, "Lord, have mercy upon me, a sinner?" Well, then, as true as the text is in the Bible, you shall have honor by-and-by. "Such honor have all the saints."

You shall have honor soon to be washed from all your guilt. You shall have honor soon to be clothed in the robes of Jesus, in the royal garments of the King. You shall have honor soon to be adopted into His family, to be received among the blood-washed ones who have been justified by faith. You shall have honor to be borne as on eagles' wings, to be carried across the river and at last to sing His praise, who has been the "death of deaths, and hell's destruction." You shall have honor to wear the crown and wave the palm one day, for you have now that humility which comes from God. You may fear that because you are now humbled by God, you must perish. I beseech you do not think so. As truly as ever the Lord has humbled you, He will exalt you. And the more you are brought low, the more hope you have of mercy. The more you are in the dust, so much the more reason you have to hope.

So far from the bottom of the sea being a place over which we cannot be carried to heaven, it is one of the nearest places to heaven's gate. And if you are brought to the very lowest place to which even Jonah descended, you are so much the nearer being accepted. The more you know your vileness—remember the blacker, the more filthy, the more unworthy you are in your own esteem—so much the more right have you to expect that you will be saved. Verily, honor shall come after humility. Humble souls, rejoice. Proud souls, go on in your proud ways, but know that they end in destruction. Climb up the ladder of your pride, you shall fall over on the other side and be dashed to pieces. Ascend the steep hill of your glory; the higher you climb the more terrible will be your fall. For know you this, that against none has the Lord Almighty bent His bow more often, and against none has He shot His arrows more furiously than against the proud and mighty man that exalts himself. Bow down, O man, bow down. "Kiss the Son, lest he be angry, and ye perish from the way, when his wrath is kindled but a little. Blessed are all they that put their trust in him."